WHY *God* LOVES US...

D1247911

WHY *God* LOVES US...

No Matter What

KEN SEDLAK, C.Ss.R.

Liguori
LIGUORI, MISSOURI

Imprimi Potest:
Thomas D. Picton, C.Ss.R.
Provincial, Denver Province
The Redemptorists

Published by Liguori Publications
Liguori, Missouri
www.liguori.org

Library of Congress Cataloging-in-Publication Data

Sedlak, Ken.
    Why God loves us...no matter what / Ken Sedlak.—1st ed.
        p. cm.
    ISBN 978-0-7648-1627-7
    1. Spirituality—Catholic Church. 2. Identity (Psychology)—Religious aspects—Christianity. 3. God—Love. I. Title
    BX2350.65.S435 2007
    248.4'82—dc22   2007011132

Scripture citations are taken from the *New Revised Standard Version* of the Bible, copyright 1989 by the Division of Christian Education of the National Council of Churches of Christ in the USA. All rights reserved. Used with permission.

Liguori Publications, a nonprofit corporation, is an apostolate of the Redemptorists. To learn more about the Redemptorists Congregation, visit *Redemptorists.com.*

Printed in the United States of America
11 10 09 08 07   5 4 3 2 1
First edition

To George and Helen Sedlak
You made love real

Contents

Preface:
The Secret
of Spirituality

There is a secret hidden in the gospels. It is a secret, not in the sense of something withheld from us, but in the sense of something that cannot be learned from others. The gospels can only point to it until we get the point for ourselves.

Jesus tells the secret in this way: "For those who want to save their life will lose it, and those who lose their life for my sake will find it" (Matthew 16:25). Concepts and ideas can only point to this self that we have to lose and this self we have to find. We must experience it as our own before it has any meaning for us.

This self is who we are before our minds create the words and images that we use to describe our self. It is us being held in existence by God. It is us as unconditional awareness and energy freely pouring out for the good of others. It is us as love—love *for* us and love *as* us.

If you want to experience this secret self as your own reality, all you need to do is ask yourself these simple questions: "Who is aware of the words on this page?" and "Who is aware that I am reading these words?" Your secret self is the awareness. Now you know. This book will help you understand the meaning and immense practicality of knowing this secret.

Introduction

Welcome!

I have thought of you often as I worked on this book. I wondered who would be attracted to this book and what cares and concerns we share.

I believe we share a desire for something that is more than temporary indulgence. We live enshrined by mystery and entranced with illusion. We are drawn to satisfy a need that is beyond our grasp. And yet we are so easily distracted.

The Scriptures try to keep us focused on what is truly important: "God's love was revealed among us in this way: God sent his only Son into the world so that we might live through him. In this is love, not that we loved God but that he loved us and sent his Son to be the atoning sacrifice for our sins. Beloved, since God loved us so much, we also ought to love one another" (1 John 4:9–11).

The stark and startling revelation is this: we exist and are held in being because God loves us. This means that when we try to understand ourselves, when we ask "Who am I?" we must more accurately ask, "Whose am I?"

I am, you are, we are the outpouring of love. We are loved absolutely and unconditionally or we would not exist.

Spirituality is about letting this reality permeate every aspect of our being, psyche, understanding, and experience. We know that this has happened when we love God, ourselves, one another, and all creation unconditionally. It has soaked our whole human reality with love, and we are free to love as we are loved.

When this reality is not absorbed, we feel isolated, frightened, defensive, angry, empty, judgmental, and meaningless. The familiarity of these feelings suggests that we have a long way to go before our subjective experience expresses our objective reality.

The founder of the Redemptorists, Saint Alphonsus Liguori, wrote: "For God, heaven is the human heart. Does God love you? Love him. His delights are to be with you; let yours be to be with him; to pass all your lifetime with him in the delight of whose company you hope to spend a blissful eternity. Accustom yourself to speak with him alone, familiarly, with confidence and love, as to the dearest friend you have, and who loves you best."[1]

This quotation has been a source of comfort, hope, and frustration for me. It is comforting and hopeful because it affirms what I most deeply desire from God, unconditional love. But it is also frustrating because I find it so hard to let God's love warm the frigid fear and anger and disease of my life. It leaves me wondering "why is it so hard to let unconditional love into our lives?" One reason, of course, is that we have talked of God's love mostly in conditional terms. We are all familiar with the image of God as the one who punishes and rewards our actions. Growing up as kids, we know that reward and punishment are facts of life. Love is very clearly conditional.

Now that we're no longer children, now that we "know better," we can still be burdened with that childhood image of God. Knowing the possibility of a healthier and more attractive image and choosing to accept that image does not seem to be enough. If we believe that love is essential to our lives, then finding a way to experience God as unconditional love is the only possibility for our healing and being truly loving ourselves.

Saint Alphonsus Liguori, in his practical and compassionate way, recommended that we meditate on three concrete realities of God's love: the crib of Christ, the cross of Christ, and the Eucharist. However, like a finger of a wise and holy guide pointing at the moon, these do little good until we look at them for ourselves.

This book is an invitation to look together.

During my lifetime I have enjoyed the companionship of many "explorers" along sacred paths. Faith, a deep and trusting awareness of the loving God, is caught, not taught. I hope to share some of what has caught me.

KEN SEDLAK, C.Ss.R.

chapter 1

Spirituality:
Knowing Who We Are
Because of Who God Is

*A*t a time in my life when I was terribly self-conscious, I came across this observation: People stand around a water cooler wondering what everybody else is thinking of them, not knowing that everybody else is also wondering what everybody else is thinking of them.

What a relief. It turned my self-conscious little fishbowl into a lake. Jesus used parables to do the same thing, to awaken us to the expansive world of God's presence as unconditional love.

Here is a parable we have heard often:

> ...[T]he kingdom of heaven is like a merchant in search of fine pearls; on finding one pearl of great value, he went and sold all that he had and bought it.
>
> MATTHEW 13:45–46

The change that this parable envisions is like relocating a goldfish from a tiny little fishbowl to Lake Michigan. Truth be known, we're used to our fishbowl. It is comfortable and familiar. So what if the bottom is made of blue pebbles, accented by a plastic castle and fake seaweed. They are our pebbles, our castle, and our fake seaweed, and we have gotten used to them. But God has created us to share in divine joy, which Jesus calls "the kingdom of God." Anything less leaves us frustrated, deaf to the words of love that will truly satisfy us, and blindly grasping for more.

Since we've lived in our little fishbowl most of our lives, we don't have a clue about what God is making possible for our lives.

In the dining room at Saint Michael's in "Old Town" Chicago, where I live, we have a *Betta* fish. He's a beautiful fish with iridescent colors and feathery fins. He also needs very little care and can survive in almost any environment. He makes a good bachelor, which is convenient because he is so aggressive that he attacks any other fish he encounters. This makes him a perfect resident in the kind of fishbowl envisioned by the traditional interpretation of this parable.

When we're honest about ourselves we may realize that we, too, are living in our own little fishbowl. There is a guardedness around our hearts, as if we're protecting ourselves. We guard ourselves against being vulnerable to life and to one another. We ache to connect with life, with someone who can love us, and with God. But we feel separate, trapped in a fishbowl.

Here's the good news Jesus came to reveal through his life: The separation we experience is an illusion that we have learned to create for ourselves. The illusion creates the knot of fear and anxiety we feel so much of the time. There is a way out of our fishbowl.

Jesus' parable breaks the illusion by awakening us to God's loving and intimate presence at the center of our being. The illusion—the feeling of isolation and separation—is created by believing that we must be the center of our lives. Look at the parable again; I'll bet you see yourself as the merchant. It's up to you to pay a great price for the pearl. Somehow you have to obtain God's presence and love for your life.

Happily, Jesus has a different vision and version of our

lives. For Jesus, God is the center of our lives, and a parable is like a good joke. Its punch line is meant to catch us off-guard and shatter the confines of our fishbowl with the surprising presence of God loving us unconditionally. If you want to "get" the punch line, you have to realize that God, not us, is the merchant, the central character in the parable. That makes us the pearl!

Could our God possibly give all that he has for our hearts? Yet isn't that what Jesus is about? "God's love was revealed among us in this way: God sent his only Son into the world so that we might live through him" (1 John 4:9).

A Zen story describes the change encountered when the reality of God's love sinks in and we are moved from our fishbowls into the life-giving waters of the kingdom of God.

God is our water. We are so used to being loved into existence that we are no longer aware of who we really are. Spirituality is about coming to know who we are because of who God is. God is our life source, intimate to every aspect of our being. We can't get away from God, let alone live or love without God. We are loved into existence and intimately united with God at every moment of our life. God is so much a part of our lives that we are no longer aware that we're immersed in God's being.

Other names for this deepest reality of our selves are *Christ Self, Heart, Divine Self, Transcendent Self, Soul, True Identity, Being, Original Face, big self, Image of God, Self, inner teacher* or *inner light, spark of the divine, spark of the soul, interior castle, foundation,* and *Higher Self.* To understand the meaning of who we truly are, we must look at God in whose image we are created.

Love Is Our Identity

"In this is love, not that we loved God but that he loved us... We love [God] because he first loved us" (1 John 4:10, 19).

The primary attribute of God in the Scriptures is love. God's nature is to give and withhold nothing, and it is by an outpouring of God's own being, God as love, that we exist at every moment.

In religion we have often talked about a loving God, but in effect we have limited God's love by what we said and did and prayed and imagined God to be. The God who punishes and rewards us to secure our obedience certainly has strong roots in tradition. As children growing up we know that reward and punishment are facts of life. At that time in our lives love is very clearly conditional.

For many of us this remains our predominant image of love. However, there has always been a parallel tradition that focuses on the unconditional nature of God's loving presence as our source. This image of God envisions a different way of understanding who God is and who we are.

In this tradition God is to reality what fire is to a flame, or the ocean to a drop of water, or a singer to the song. God is not someone distinct from what is but Being in which all beings participate. God is both the vastness of the universe and the intimacy of our person. God is the reality of all that is real, and the luminous source radiating all that is living.

Just as God cannot be limited, neither can God's nature. God is unconditional and unmediated love. God pours out his own personal being as creation. God loves us into existence unconditionally, person to person. This is not an abstract gen-

> I, the fiery life of Divine essence, am aflame beyond the beauty of the meadows, I gleam in the waters, I burn in the sun, moon and stars. With every breeze, as with invisible life that embraces everything, I awaken all creatures to life...
> I am the breeze that nurtures all things green.
> I encourage blossoms to flourish with ripening fruits,
> I am the rain coming from the dew that causes the grasses to laugh with the joy of life.
> Hildegard of Bingen[1]

eralization, but personal love, God's self-existence pouring itself out as my existence, your existence, and all existence. God knows us for who we are because God has chosen to create us. God knows you for who you are and is choosing to love you into existence at this very moment.

Our Human Dilemma: Loved and Wounded

We are the "beloved child" of God, a continuation of love. This is not an identity we choose, but one we find to be ours as we let go of all the partial identities and qualities we use to describe ourselves. This is God's gift, freely given for my sake, and your sake. As a free gift, it is given unconditionally because this gives us the freedom of a subject, it makes us a person. God's love does not turn us into an object of God's agenda. It is freely given and giving freedom. That's the only way we could love in return.

At this point, let me say that I know as well as you that this is not my experience of myself. I do not experience myself as being able to freely give love. However, I am also aware that I yearn, in Gerald G. May's phrase, "for action that does not mimic love, but springs forth from love."[2] I wish I could love this freely and this generously.

A friend and I once gave a retreat to a group of monks. Trying to gain some insight into the group, we talked to their abbot. He summarized his brothers this way, "They are good men with even better intentions." I want to believe that my best intentions are as much a part of me as my most addictive behaviors. I find myself far less loving and more self-centered than I wish to be. Because of this I believe something else must be at play in our lives.

Our dogma professor, Father Gerry Owens, C.Ss.R., used to say that original sin is the "most obvious of all our beliefs." This is what is at play in our lives. Here is Thomas Keating's description:

The fact is, we are all in desperate need of happiness and don't know where it can be found. This teaching is classical in the Christian tradition and is described in theology as the consequences of original sin...The first consequence of original sin, according to traditional theology is illusion. We don't know what true happiness is or where it is to be found. The second consequence is concupiscence. Since we are made for boundless happiness, we have to find it somewhere and not knowing where to find it, we look for it in the wrong places. And third, we suffer from weakness of will, which means that even if someday we discover where true happiness is to be found, our will is too weak to do anything about it. This is why we need to be redeemed.[3]

The good news is that something is being done, even before we become aware of our need. Redemption is being done, even before we know what we want. Redemption is a way of saying that God pours out love, not only as our existence, but also as our healing. And it is God's joy when we choose to participate in accepting this creative love.

In Ron Hanson's beautifully written book, *Mariette in Ecstasy*, we come to know Mariette as a young woman who is totally in love with Jesus. She enters a convent as a way of giving herself to her lover, but her presence becomes disruptive to the life of the convent and eventually she is asked to leave. Many years later we come upon her writing to an old classmate from her convent days. She still burns with an intimate love for Christ as her own words so beautifully express:

And Christ still sends me roses. We try to be formed and held and kept by him, but instead he offers us freedom. And now when I try to know his will, his kindness floods me, his great love overwhelms me, and I hear him whisper, "Surprise me."[4]

God creates us, not as mimics of God's love, but as free and creative agents. In love with us, God creates us as the possibility of responding with the same love for God and all God's creation. God creates us so that we can relate to God and one another. The creator of the entire universe, the source of all reality, pours out being as our being, so that we can relate person to person, subject to subject, creature to Creator. We have the possibility of loving God as our gift of ourselves.

> *The freedom question, then, is not whether we can do whatever we want but whether we can do what we most deeply want....*
>
> Gerald G. May[5]

This is who we are. Because of who God is, we are loved and loving. This is our essence. This is what we must learn to express through our living if we want to know meaning and fulfillment and the happiness we are created to share with God.

The Freedom to Love Another for Who They Are

To love means to see a person as he or she really is, not as we imagine him or her to be. And to respond to that person in a way that recognizes his or her true value, freedom, and subjectivity. God loves us as the limited and wounded human beings that we are.

At the same time, God knows our potential and makes a place for us to be partners in creation. Maybe it's just natural for a loving creator and artist to want to share the joy of creating. We are invited into a relationship of intimacy, friendship, and partnership.

When I was finishing theology studies in the Hudson

Valley of New York, my friend Paul and I were in charge of decorating the chapel for Christmas. Just before Thanksgiving we got the figures out for the crib so that we could clean them. Unfortunately, I dropped Baby Jesus and chipped his nose. The figures were from Italy and there was no way we could replace Jesus before Christmas. We were taking an art course at the time and decided to sculpt our own figures. It was a busy time and we worked whenever we had a few minutes, and rarely together. Paul worked on Joseph, I worked on Mary, and we kept the figures covered with wet cloth so that the clay would not dry up.

Paul is effervescent and outgoing, I tend to be reticent and introverted. Without knowing it, our personalities affected our approach to creating our sculptures. Paul, who was working on Saint Joseph, started small and added bit by bit. I started with a large mound of clay and whittled it down to form Mary. Joseph ended up being two feet high and Mary eight inches—and neither was much to look at. But we were proud. They were beautiful in our eyes. We had invested our hearts in them.

Doesn't something like this happen with parents? They love their child who can provide no self-care, who has not succeeded at anything or garnered any prestige. Yet they love their child, because the child is their creation. There is joy and pride in creating, and we are offered a share in our Creator's joy. I remember when my sister Karen had Jeffery, her first baby. She was so excited, so proud. He just laid there. The first time Jeffery smiled, we all felt that we had been blessed by God. Imagine how God must love you, so much that God continues to love you into existence at this very moment.

Idolatry Is Trying to Use God

God loves us unconditionally even though we have not acted lovingly, and he forgives us even before we seek forgiveness.

If there is a downside to this, from the human point of view, it is that we can no more make God an object of our agenda than God will make us an object of his agenda. In Scripture the opposite of faith is neither doubt nor atheism, but idolatry—turning God into an object, an idol. Idolatry is using God instead of relating to God. Meister Eckhart sums it up succinctly. "Some people want to look upon God with their eyes, as they look upon a cow, and want to love God as they love a cow. Thus they love God for the sake of external riches and of internal solace."[6] Love creates for us a relationship and love will not be used by us.

Is love enough? Even if it means losing some cherished notions of God? Instead of a God who "watches over us," we now have a God who keeps watch *with* us. Instead of a God who is ready in the wings to rescue us, we have "the wind beneath our wings." Instead of a God with a well-mapped-out plan that we have to "discern," we have a God who invites us to participate in creating the plan itself, a shared future.

> There is only one problem on which all my existence, my peace, and my happiness depend: to discover myself in discovering God. If I find him I will find myself and if I find my true self I will find him.
>
> Thomas Merton[7]

If love is enough, if you know that deep hunger within you to be loved and to be loving, then you might wonder what stands between you and experiencing the immediacy of God's presence? If you are ready to relate to God because you *want to*, rather than because you *have to*, then you may be wondering what you need to do to let God come close.

Our Secret Self, Our True Self, Our Identity

Once again we return to the secret hidden in the gospels. It is one that the spiritual masters know about, one that Jesus struggled to share with his disciples and struggles to share with us. When we know it, all those passages in the gospels that seem so obtuse begin to make sense. As I mentioned, it is a secret, not in the sense of something withheld from us, but in the sense of something that cannot be learned from others. They can only point to it until we get the point for ourselves. Thomas Merton's phrase for this is "true self." As I mentioned previously, there are many other words or phrases for this, such as *Christ Self, Heart, Divine Self, Transcendent Self, Soul, True Identity, Being, Original Face, Image of God, Self.*

The true self is who we are before our judgments and perceptions distort our awareness. It is unconditional awareness. Our true self is energy freely poured out to others. It is love. The true self is our being as an expression of God's being. It is pure being, without thoughts, emotions, or sensations.

Knowing the True Self as Our Truth

I, my true self, my very being, the part of me who is always here, is an expression of God's love.

Knowing about God's love and our true self is not enough. To know it as our own truth means understanding how we create our sense of identity, who we believe ourselves to be. When we come to know that the identity our mind creates is only partial, then we can let go of our partial identity in favor of the fullness of who we are. We can let go of the distraction that is our ego and experience who we really are, the person who is loved and loving.

In self-help literature the primary prescription for feeling better about ourselves is "Take two affirmations and get a good night's sleep." We all need to be affirmed. No one of us has been loved unconditionally by the people we grew up with. And even if we have, the way our sense of self develops is by choosing qualities and rejecting others within ourselves. That leaves us wounded (what traditional theology calls "original sin"). We feel cut off from the source of our being.

We feel separated from the foundation of our heart, looking to externals to bolster our vulnerability. To compensate we create an identity composed of partial truths, none of which can express or bear the significance of our unique person. We are orphans who have wandered away from our divine heritage, which is the only possible source of true happiness, peace, and identity. Still worse, we have forgotten who we are—the wonderful mystery of a self held in existence by unconditional love.

I was in New Orleans one summer when a hurricane struck. Luckily we were in a house that had already withstood a hundred years of hurricanes. All we had to do was latch the shutters and sit tight. The hurricane blew all around us. The trees bent in obedience to its power, and rain attacked horizontally. The intensity of the winds swelled, the house heaved, and the electricity went out. In the darkness we could see the lightning hammer out the shapes of houses around us. Our house shivered, the windows chattered, and then, silence. We entered the eye of the storm.

The true self is the silence and calm at the center of our storm. Around this center, however, powerful energies spin. The outer winds consist of all the activities and events going on around us—things of national concern, incidents at work, and encounters in our relationships. There is so much happening and so many things with which we must deal.

The inner winds are filled with the turmoil of our inner world: emotions, thoughts, physical sensations, memories, and patterns of reacting. Close your eyes for a moment and you become aware of what Buddhists call the "drunken monkey," swinging from thought to thought, image to image, emotion to emotion, and back again. Our inner world literally has a mind of its own. When we begin to pay attention to it, we often feel helpless. These thoughts and emotions are fed by energies as vast as earth's own weather systems. No wonder they get our attention.

This is why it is so difficult to believe that we exist on a deeper level, let alone experience living from that level. Our attention is absorbed in dealing with the energy and commotion of those outer levels. It is just common sense to take care of business and that leaves little time or energy for seeking something as seemingly exotic as a "true self." Those who have been there know differently.

> ..."[D]o not keep striving for what you are to eat and what you are to drink, and do not keep worrying. For it is the nations of the world that strive after all these things, and your Father knows that you need them. Instead, strive for his kingdom, and these things will be given you as well.
> "Do not be afraid, little flock, for it is your Father's good pleasure to give you the kingdom."
>
> LUKE 12:29–32

The kingdom of God is within; it is the eye of the hurricane. Yet all this remains abstract, pretty words, poetry at best, until we begin to know it for ourselves. Prayer, meditation, silence, letting go of our judgments and opinions, living in the present moment, dream work, focusing, and keeping a journal are just a few ways the kingdom becomes real. In my life prayer and meditation have been essential because they plunge me into the reality of God.

Experiences of Our True Self

I am personally convinced that understanding our true self as a deeper reality than our mind and ego is tremendously helpful along the spiritual path. I emphasize *personally* because whenever I talk about this, it seems to evaporate before it makes contact with the people to whom I'm talking. I believe that this is true because we cannot put our true selves into words. It's the "you" and the "me" that exist consistently through all the physical, emotional, mental, and external changes we have experienced. It is the love and unconditional awareness that we are, before we began to use these concepts to represent our self as an ego.

Here is a quick experiment that can help you get in touch with your reality as true self. As you sit reading these words, take a few moments to close your eyes and come fully into this moment. Take a few deep breaths and let all the ideas, thoughts, and conversations swirling around in your head flow out of you as you exhale. Breathe slowly and deeply, and you will relax...slowly and deeply.

You can see the print on this page. It is seen, right? But seen by whom? In this very moment, outside of memories or concepts or images, who is seeing? Shift your attention from the words on the page back to yourself. Be attentive to whatever comes into your awareness. Maybe thoughts and feelings come into your awareness. You are aware of them. Shift back to yourself. Who is aware of these thoughts and feelings?

> *In diligent exercise of mystical contemplation, leave behind the senses and the operations of the intellect, and all things sensible and intellectual, and all things in the world of being and non-being, that you may arise by unknowing towards the union...with him who transcends all being and all knowledge.*
>
> Dionysius the Areopagite[8]

If a word comes in response to this last question, ask yourself again, *who* is aware of this word? Whenever something comes into your awareness, ask yourself, "*Who* is aware?"

You may begin to experience—beyond all the ideas, memories, feelings, and physical sensations going on within you—a mysterious presence, indefinable, with the capacity to be present to everything just exactly as it is. This presence contains your body but exists beyond your body. It contains your thoughts and emotions and all the qualities you call *you*, but exists beyond them, as awareness of them. This presence is your awareness prior to thought, the space in which the thought—or emotion, memory, sense perception—happens. This presence is you as awareness, as true self. You can't reflect back on it, you can only experience being present and aware.

I'm going to describe some of the experiences that are experiences of our true self. Some of us will be more familiar with one experience rather than another. I'll put the basic experience in **bold** and you can look for the one that grabs your attention. Their value is not in giving you information, but in helping you become aware that you exist beyond all the thoughts and sensations you have identified as being you.

• **Who's talking inside of my head?** When I was about seven years old, I remember asking my mother, "Are there two people inside of me?" She looked a little taken back, but gamely asked, "Why do you ask?"

"Because," I said, "I can listen to me talking inside of my head."

"Don't tell anybody," she said, "they'll think you're crazy."

And that was that, at least for a while. But yes, we can be aware of ourselves thinking. When we begin to pay attention to the workings of the mind, it seems to have a life of its own. When I first realized that my mind was generating much of the anxiety I felt about so many simple tasks, I was astounded. It was like my mind was working against me. And it can do that until we become aware of its games. Our mind works as a filter, using old memories and patterns to interpret our present experience. There is hope when we become aware of this, hope that we will no longer be blinded to our blindness. But even more than that, hope that we can know ourselves as more than our mind, more than the images through which our minds see, more than our judgments and opinions.

When we begin to watch our minds at work, we come to know ourselves as more than our mind. When we become aware of the patterns of thought that continually replicate themselves in our mind, we realize that we are more than those patterns. When we catch ourselves creating anxiety, we find that we are more than our anxiety. We know our knowing. We are more than the content of our mind. In fact, we are a deep center of pure awareness and unconditional love. We share the genes of our Creator.

• **I'm not satisfied with what I have, and what I want isn't enough either.** We desire to be loved and to be loving. "The heart yearns in simple, silent pleading for action that does not mimic love but springs forth from it...."[10] I requote these words from The Awakened Heart because they send shivers of recognition through my heart. They wrap words around an intuition that has been struggling for awareness for as long as I can remember.

> *For the most part all our trials and disturbances come from our not understanding ourselves.*
> Saint Teresa of Ávila[9]

If we follow the lead of our desires, we will find that they are echoes of our deep nature, our true self, which is held in existence by unconditional love. Think for a moment about what has prompted you to do what you have done in your life. When you have tried to be successful, what have you been seeking? When you have wanted to be pleasing, attractive, or helpful to others, what have you really been hoping for? Our deepest desire is to be loved and loving.

Most often we experience this desire as frustration or an exquisite longing. We feel restless, never fully satisfied and with no idea what will satisfy us. There's an emptiness in the pit of our being that cannot be filled. We hunger but nothing is appetizing; or we can be prodded by the possibility of enchantment, the promise of completion, and the intuition of a secret treasure hidden just beyond our grasp. If we look closely, we see that every choice is driven by the need to find an antidote for this restless desire. Sooner or later we might begin to wonder if anything can truly satisfy us.

At the same time, to have a longing is to sense that it *can* be satisfied; that something does exist to quell its compulsion.

> *We love because he first loved us.*
> 1 John 4:19
> _____
> *We desire because we have been desired.*
> Alphonsus Liguori[11]

We are truly blessed when we discover in this desire our thirst for God. We are even more blessed when we realize that this desire exists because we are desired by God. The source of our desire is God's desire for us.

We have so many loves—we have fallen for so many things—that we are only dimly aware of what we're seeking. We hunger for satisfaction, for real fulfillment. Not finding it, we stuff ourselves with food and stuff our houses with gadgets and furnishings. Unfortunately, these distractions entice us into settling for much less.

There is an old vaudeville joke that is to the point. A man goes to the doctor and says, "Doctor, my wife is crazy. She thinks she's a chicken." "How do you know she thinks she's a chicken?" the doctor asks. "Because she walks around clucking, and bobbing, and eating corn meal just like a chicken does," the husband said. "Why don't you bring her in and I'll see what I can do?" the doctor suggests. "I would," the husband says, "but I need the eggs."

It's hard to let go of the symptoms when we think the product is something we desire. Following desire's lead can awaken us, in a roundabout way, to desire's source. That's why Saint Alphonsus promoted prayer of petition so passionately. As we encounter the silence of God, we find our own voice in these petitions and sort out our desires as we begin to look for lasting satisfaction. Desire is our true self calling us home.

- **I know I'm me, but I can't explain what that means.**

What if I ask you to tell me a little about yourself, who you are? What is it that makes you *you*?

Think about all the words you would use to describe yourself. None of them is essential to you—they all change. Your job has changed. Where you live has changed. The sound of your voice has changed. Every cell in your body changes every seven years. Think how many times you've changed your mind. Yet something uniquely you remains. With all this change you still know that you are the same person at forty that you were at age four.

At the same time that "something uniquely you (that) remains" is more than any of the words you use to describe yourself.

If you live in a big city, you know that whenever you try to walk from one place to another you will run into "street people." You wouldn't be out on the streets if you didn't have something to do. And that means that when they try to stop you for some change, or a couple of bucks for a bus fare, you're going to feel interrupted and intruded upon. But there are those times when something breaks through and you see them no longer as an "interruption" but as individual persons. You have a sense that comes from beyond being politically correct that in their own unique way, they share humanity with you. "Street people," "Interruption," "Intruder"—any label, even the most benevolent, feels like a lie. This is a person, and no label, no word, describes who he or she is. We share something that cannot be put into words.

For a moment, something has taken us beyond our fears and suspicions. We are aware that what we share is nobler than the circumstances of our lives. This is different than pity, which comes mostly from our head and our judgments and is often fueled with guilt. Instead, we respond person-to-person. It's a somewhat vulnerable time, but that doesn't seem to matter. It's as if, for a moment, we don't have to worry about protecting our fragile egos. We feel an inner freedom to be our self.

• **Something beyond me has helped me survive the worst times of my life.** Can you remember a time when your desire no longer felt chaotic, tumultuous, and chronically unsatisfied? Instead, you were soothed by something from deep inside, and you felt focused, at peace and clear, aware of life living within you.

Sometimes this happens at difficult and negative times in our lives. At times of loss, we become frightfully aware that all the things that seemed to matter no longer do, and that their loss makes us feel more real and more alive than we normally feel. When we lose our job or break up a relationship, we are thrown into chaos. And yet, in the midst of this turmoil, we may gradually become aware of something alive within us. It's like a blade of grass has sprung up in our inner desert. The world, which has gone its merry way without us, begins to have a place for us once more. The surprise is that this new surge of life happens to us, not because of anything we have done, and at times, despite all that we have done. New life is being given from a source beyond our control. In our helplessness, we realize that we are being helped.

A friend of mine, deeply grieving the loss of both her mother and sister, had this surprising comment about her grief. She talked about how her grief comes in waves and comes at times when she least expects it. Often the grief is overwhelming and feels as though it is crushing her. At other times it drains her energy, leaving her depressed, angry, and feeling helpless. Yet in the midst of all this turmoil, she says she feels alive in a way "I've never felt before. I feel like I'm more truly myself, more authentic than I've ever been." Something is alive about her that she does not cause or control. She has the feeling of life being given her, an energetic aliveness that is uncrushable, that shines through her darkest moments. It is like that blade of grass sprouting in the middle of the desert. It doesn't seem like much, but it is there and is vibrantly alive. And it is her more truly than all the pain.

These are moments when our true self bursts into awareness. Just briefly, we know what it's like to be a daughter or son of God. We know this not as privilege, nor as arrogance, but as the simple, unadorned reality of being loved into existence.

How Can This Have Happened?

One Christmas Eve I went with some friends, "Grandma and Grandpa," to watch their grandson Patrick open his gifts. It was the first time Christmas really meant something to him, and they came over to watch someone they loved enjoy his gifts. Around 9:00 PM there was a pounding on the front door and a "Ho, ho, ho." The noise terrified Patrick and in a panic he looked for his Dad, who wasn't there. His mother opened the door to reveal Santa Claus and Patrick hid behind Grandma. Santa brought in a gift for him, an easel for drawing and painting. It had its own little chair, and crayons, pastels, and paints so that Patrick could draw to his heart's delight. And as soon as Santa left, he became totally engrossed in his art. The rest of us exchanged gifts and then it was time for Patrick to open the rest of his gifts. After all, that's what we were there for: to share his joy. But he was already enjoying all that he needed and he didn't want anything else. Unfortunately, there were more gifts to open. His parents were in a bind, and when they tried to get him to open the gifts he cried and had a fit. He just wanted to be left alone with his easel. With a lot of love and the best of intentions we, in effect, were trying to get him to ignore his heart's desire so that we could give him more "heart's desires." Sooner or later, each one of us loses our heart's desire in a deluge of options.

We are created by Love to be loved unconditionally. We

end up, however, settling for much less. Instead of experiencing our true identity as beloved children of God, we become identified with externals. Our identity, who we sense ourselves to be, becomes linked with objects and descriptions of ourselves. We feel important because we have the right car, or because we are called by a respected title, or because someone thinks we're "nice." A cartoon in today's paper shows two young girls talking about boys. One advises the other, "All you have to do is go up to one, touch his arm, and say 'My, have you been working out?' "

We identify our self with qualities, with the things that can be said about us in comparison to others—that we are more muscular, taller or handsomer, smarter or richer, more caring, or members of this group as opposed to that group—or whatever. When we identify, get our sense of self from a quality, we also begin to feel that anything that lessens the identification of this quality with us diminishes our self, our sense of "me."

We can look to just about anything for our value, our sense of esteem, and our security. We become attached to them. When they are threatened, we feel threatened. In any case, we lose awareness of God as the true Source of our self, our identity, and our security.

Our desire to be loved unconditionally and to love freely in return is short-circuited by the fear and anxiety that come from the possibility of losing these external descriptions and objects. We feel better about ourselves because of our position at work, the kind of neighborhood in which we live, or the type of car we drive. And we feel worse about ourselves—threatened—when we feel that any of these are threatened.

The object of our attachment may be anything: a person, a place, a substance, a behavior, or a belief. We can identify with things as great as faithfulness to our family or allegiance to our country, or as small as keeping a new car unscratched.

We can be compelled by things as noble as peace and justice or as petty as power and greed. And most often, all these are mixed together. We can even turn God into an object of attachment when we try to use God for our own ends. We try to make God an accomplice in our anxiety-driven agendas. Out of habit we turn God into an object and reduce God to the limits of our ego and mind.

As previously mentioned, the opposite of faith is neither atheism nor doubt, but idolatry. When God is no longer first in our lives, everything else is in disarray. We begin to experience ourselves as separate individuals, "on our own." The objects and descriptions with which we identify have to fill in for God. We feel angry when we perceive that they are threatened and hurt when their value is not shared by others. This makes us feel we need to insist on getting our way as a means of defending our existence and our description.

This leads to judging everything according to whether it is good or bad for me as a private, separate individual. We protect our advantage from others seeking to gain their own advantage. We see ourselves as separated beings, fragments that relate to other fragments. Our life becomes self-defensive and necessarily selfish. We are fighting for survival because we have lost the security of our eternal and mutual Source.

At the beginning of this chapter I mentioned my reaction when I found that everybody else was worried about what everybody else was thinking about them. It was a relief to be released from my self-imposed fishbowl to swim in the vast waters of humanity—but it also brought a new kind of anxiety. If I'm just one among many, who am I? I need to stand out in some way, to be unique, to have my own identity. I have to separate myself from the rest of the crowd. This is basic to how our minds work every moment of every day. Everything is always dualistic; we can frame reality only in terms of "either/or." The mind reads every situation in terms of who is right and who is wrong.

To be me means I have to judge you for being different than me. I need *my* qualities to be exclusively mine. Most often I judge you as being less than me, although perversely, I sometimes need you to be more than me so that I can rely on you. This is a way of using you as my strength. In any case, I am reducing both of us to labels much smaller than the persons we are.

More insidiously, I need to keep you in your place to feel secure in mine. As a newly ordained priest, I was asked to give a retreat at a women's retreat house in Tacoma, Washington. Being newly ordained is a privileged time in life. People are so happy to see youth and new energy that all you have to do is show up in a black shirt and white collar and you are treated as a "little less than the gods." What I didn't know was that part of the job description is repeating what we always learned and not straying from the security of the familiar. The retreat started Friday night. When I went to breakfast Saturday morning, the Mother Superior of the retreat house was waiting for me. "Some of the women have been up all night because of your remarks. They're threatening to call the bishop."

Well, that led to an open forum to find out what I said that was so upsetting. At this time, Vatican II was just starting to be implemented and maybe some of the "new changes" were upsetting. Finally, one of the women stood up: "Father, last night you flippantly said we cannot merit heaven. I've spent my whole life trying to be a good Catholic so that I could merit heaven. Are you trying to tell me that I don't have a chance and my whole life is a waste?"

I had paraphrased Saint Teresa of Ávila, who said we don't *need to merit* God's love—it's a gift that we don't win or lose. God's joy is to love us. To this woman, however, this was not just an idea among many; it was a dismantling of her identity, value, and hope for life after this world. She had reason to be angry at me. In her mind, my role as a priest was to comfort her with what she wanted to hear and I had betrayed her.

This dynamic of identifying ourselves with descriptions and external objects is the source of many of our troubles. In this simple, innocent, and unconscious choice, we have turned to externals as our source of esteem, power, and security. Any perceived threat to these leaves us angry, fearful, and anxious. At the very least, it leads us to treat one another as objects. You have value to me so long as you fit into my plans.

And you become less than human when you do something to frustrate my desire for approval and admiration. Now you are a threat, and I have a whole series of judgments for people who threaten whatever I feel makes me feel secure. If you stop me from having things go my way, you will face my anger and disgust. I feel I have a right to think well of myself and to be angry in defense of myself. I need things to be my way, and anything that upsets that is wrong.

A better way of life is possible, however. The spiritual traditions of all great world religions have developed methods to shift from the limited and defensive self to our true self. Jesus clearly worked out of this self-awareness. His teaching and actions were meant to awaken his disciples, and us, to its reality.

If I'm Not Me, Who Am I?

If I'm not the voice in my head—that ongoing monologue that comments, compares, likes and dislikes, and then worries— then who am I? If I am not my descriptions, feelings, body, or external objects, what is left? The answer might be better than you would think. Here's how to find out. Take a couple of deep breaths, let yourself relax, let your thoughts and judgments drop away, and keep your consciousness quietly and simply on the present moment. As soon as you attend to the present moment, stress and struggles dissolve, along with your memories, anticipation and anxiety, and you simply are. Whatever you do becomes imbued with a sense of quality, ease, and love, even the simplest actions. You are no longer bound to the dissatisfactions of the past or the anxiety of a future that exists only in your defensive imagining. When you let go of "me," you are your true self, living energy and love. As soon as you try to get a hold on you, you are trapped once again in your anxieties. Since true self is essential awareness and love, it cannot reflect upon itself; our mind cannot get a hold of it. True self is the reflecting. It can only be lived as nonjudging, unconditional love and awareness. And this happens only when we let go.

> "Do not judge, so that you may not be judged. For with the judgment you make you will be judged, and the measure you give will be the measure you get."
>
> Matthew 7:1–2

On television talk shows, when they run out of topics, they do makeovers. Three or four people are chosen to have their hairstyle, makeup, and style of clothing changed. We see them before and after the change. And then they have to face that most overused of questions, "How do you feel?" They look different and they usually report feeling different—more confident, more "myself," and happy to be a new person.

My nephew, David, once convinced Jenny, his little sister, that she had super powers. Her power was this: she could run and get him soda pop and snacks at split-second speeds. He proved it with a stopwatch. And then let her time him to see how much slower he was. He gained control over her by selling her an attractive (to a five-year-old) self-image. Luckily she figured it out when she got tired of her super powers. It's easy to sell ourselves short.

Our self-image, our identity, who we imagine ourselves to be, has a powerful impact on the way we perceive ourselves and others. When we begin to experience the reality of our true self, our self-image not only changes, but is transformed. It is not just an improvement of our existing image but a radical (in the sense of reaching to our roots) shift to a new foundation for living. We are transformed from experiencing ourselves as separate and fragmented to being a subject. We lose our self to gain eternal life.

We are created by Love to be loved and to be loving. Such is the nature of the Love that creates us, is our life force, and wants to be given to others.

This is our true self, the "beloved child of God," our deepest identity. If we can spend enough time in the stillness and peace of the hurricane's eye, we will be able to bring the love and peace at the center of our self into the outer winds of our life. This is the kingdom of God that Jesus came to establish and call us into partnership. We can make it a living reality in our flesh and blood.

Who We Are Because of Who God Is

Who we are cannot be put into words.

We are nonjudgmental awareness and unconditional loving.

We are an energetic being for others.

And we are the freedom to relate to others, not as objects but as a subject in our own right.

All of this is true of us because God is unconditional love who pours out Divine Being as the source of our being.

A more accurate question than "If I'm not 'me,' who am I?" would be: "If I'm not 'me,' whose am I?"

The following chapters build on this foundation. They also explore the reality of our limitations as human beings and God's determination to heal the wound created by the development of our sense of self as separate individuals.

chapter 2

The Child in the Crib, the Gift of Our Divine Identity

Many of my hopes and dreams are rooted in my childhood memories of Christmas. Christmas was my first conscious taste of the divine, of being the recipient of something beyond my greatest imaginings. And these memories and images encourage my hope to this day.

As a child, going to church meant boredom.

"Sit still."

"Be quiet."

All this while adults did stuff that only they could appreciate. It was like being exiled to a foreign country, filled with foreign sounds, foreign colors, and foreign customs. Nothing stimulated my interest, entertained my desires, or gave hope to my dreams. It was their world, not mine.

Watching the adults go to Communion was my favorite part because it meant the monstrous monotony would end soon.

Even though Christmas Eve was decked in new colors and sounds and the air glittered with expectation, I soon found it was just camouflage for the extended rituals that stood between us and the glorious possibilities that lay wrapped in our presents at home.

Surprisingly enough, it was after being lulled into semi-consciousness at Christmas Eve Mass that Jesus first snuggled into my life. To get out of the door we had to pass by the crib. As my mother paused to point out the angels and shepherds, and Mary and Joseph, the child was looking right at me. Kid to kid we sized each other up. My first reaction was hesitant and defensive. The child's eyes established him as an equal, someone who was as clear about what he saw and what he wanted as I was. But his size and the manger made him vulnerable, waking my compassion. I felt like a new baby brother had been given to our family, one who already knew the mysteries of navigating the adult world. He was small enough to need me and smart enough that I could trust him to lead me.

It was my first conscious introduction into the wild and startling intimacy that faith unleashes.

Like a baby's first taste of ice cream. The first flavor is cold and somewhat unpleasant. I wasn't sure I liked this kid. And then the sweet creamy epiphany melts into my taste buds, and the cold is refreshing and delighting and oozing with soothing contentment. I knew he was more than a new brother; he was my twin, my companion, my comfort, and my encouragement.

I didn't know it, but on that Christmas Eve I first became aware, beyond my ability to verbalize or conceptualize it, of an intimacy with God that would fund my hopes and my bravest dreams and my reluctant steps into an adult future. In Jesus I found someone who would come into my life rather than expect me to live as a blundering guest in an alien land.

We cannot understand the crib and Incarnation in an analytical, abstract way. Each of us is welcomed into the stories and images of Advent and Christmas as tales of our own heritage and identity. The wonder of the crib or Incarnation is that God saves us by pouring divinity into our humanness.

The Word becomes Flesh, God becomes human, the darkness becomes Light; all tell us of the unconquerable God who gives himself into the vulnerability of our humanity. A God who surrenders to each one of us is the mystery of the crib. Jesus' Incarnation is linked to our becoming. Christ is born today through our rebirth.

The gospels weave a rich tapestry of images that draw us into God's imagination and his vision. As we tell and retell the story of the unexpected and marvelous birth of the Holy One among us, we experience the intimacy and the mystery of that relationship in a new way. Our relationship with Jesus grows and matures as our imagination grows and matures. Jesus, who began by snuggling up to our hearts, uses that heart to pry us open to the unrestricted grandeur of unconditional love. We are living a mystery that resonates with our deepest self and yet is always more than we can know. We intuit its reality but never grasp its breadth. Its meaning comes from the deepest level of our sense of our own reality.

Ordinarily we think of the Incarnation as God entering human life and history in the person of Jesus. But the Incarnation is also about our entering into the life of God.

> *In the beginning was the Word, and the Word was with God, and the Word was God. He was in the beginning with God. All things came into being through him, and without him not one thing came into being. What has come into being in him was life, and the life was the light of all people. The light shines in the darkness, and the darkness did not overcome it.*
>
> *JOHN 1:1–5*

Even when I was a child, this reading sent shimmers of vague recognition through me. I never heard the rest of the gospel. It seemed to trail off into a thicket of tangled words, but these words rang true even in my childish heart. They seemed vital to my welfare, as if this beginning was somehow continued in my own beginning. And in John's contemplative understanding of Jesus, this is where we are led.

The Word is the manifestation of divine being. Just as the sun and its light are two aspects of one reality, the Father and Son are one, but they are two aspects of divinity, just as a dowel rod has two ends yet remains one reality. The Son's origin is from the Father but, together they constitute one reality; one aspect reveals itself in the other.

We are included in this intimate unity. We are that flame of God's fire. We are a drop of water in God's ocean. And Jesus is the unveiling of all that is most true about us as God's finite manifestations. God as love pours out God's being, God's self as the source of all that exists. And Jesus, the Word, reveals our origin in divine being. We are not gods, but we exist as God's.

Theology talks about this as *agape love*. Metaphysics talks about it as *Being* whose nature expands in every possible way. Creation is God's love expressing itself in every possible way.

Sometimes I sit in silence. For a moment my mind is like Teflon and thoughts just slide on through. I become aware of a life force breathing within me, beating blood through my body, and energizing my awareness. Love is creating and energizing me at every moment, and I get a fleeting sense of love energy expressing itself in everything around me.

Infinite and finite are two poles of one reality, which is to say, we are part of the finite pole of infinite reality. God loves and God loves to create. We are the part of God's self-expression that is uniquely gifted with the ability to become aware of God as joyous love creating us.

As the perfect manifestation of this reality, Jesus is the word that speaks directly to our consciousness, opening it to the joyous and intimate love that is our source. Jesus expresses the silent Father's outpouring of love as the source of our lives and all of created reality.

At the same time, Jesus is the perfect expression of all that we can be in response to that love. Jesus becoming flesh is the pattern of our becoming humanly divine. We become whole by becoming God's. We are God's infinite love in the limits of this time and place. Along with Jesus we can become aware that we are divine and beloved children. He is our word also, the revealing of who we are. His gospel is our biography.

We possess a dual destiny—human and divine—and it plays itself out in every part of our lives. Think of our celebration of Christmas. It is supposed to be the feast of Jesus Christ the Incarnation of God in the world. But it has been pirated and left to drift in a swamp of consumer products. Paradoxically, as "secular" as this may be, it awakens us to our yearnings for that "something more," which is the divine.

Christmas' Gift Is Wrapped in Our Flesh

As I write this I am in Tucson, Arizona, where the December skies are bright blue and 74 degrees. Meanwhile in Chicago, where I live, they are digging out from seven inches of snow. It's so good to be here. Yet when I hear "White Christmas" at the grocery store, I'm immediately drawn into an ache for the snow that I'm so happy to have escaped.

Christmas does that. It incarnates our desires for what is missing. It helps us pay attention to the rest of our story. We usually settle for getting by, numb to the pain of frustrated deep desires. We long for a home, a place where we truly belong. And we ache for companions who can rescue us from that aloneness we feel even in crowds.

In the private, quiet moments of Christmas we sorely long for a savior. We are reminded of who we really are: human beings who are incomplete when alienated from the divine.

The tragedy is that so often we are trapped by the "incomplete" part.

Teilhard de Chardin puts the greater truth succinctly and encouragingly: "We are not human beings having a spiritual experience; we are spiritual beings having a human experience." Spirituality is about who we are because of who God is. And God is the one who incarnates to create. There is no "incomplete" part of our lives. We have already reached our goal. We exist because of divine intimacy. God is choosing us now, and now, and now. What is absent is awareness. We are restless until we come to know this as our own reality.

The good news is that the unconditioned God was born into this world just like you and me. In Jesus, divinity wrapped our wary flesh around himself and became the revelation of divine intimacy as the very source of our self. Jesus, as the incarnate togetherness of divine and human nature, guarantees in his person that intimacy with God is not only possible but actually the source of our being. Jesus is the revelation that we exist because our Father desires us and that our own desire for love will lead us to our Father.

For me, this is the wonderful irony of Christmas. Just as this feast was stolen from its Christian roots, it is reclaimed to become the possibility of our salvation. God is so intimate, so close, that whenever we scratch the surface of our awareness, we can be drawn back to our true relationship with God. Christmas stirs up our desires. When the gifts we receive fail to satisfy our true desire, the resultant frustration can lead us to our real desire and remembrance of our source in God.

As I look around my office, I see that I have collected so many things—CDs, books, knickknacks—that I never use or enjoy. Things I could live without. Like the Christmas consumer binge, they are also reminders that I crave awareness of God's intimacy. I am restless until I find my heart's desire in God.

Our own incarnation, our becoming flesh and blood, is a reliving of the pattern of the Word's Incarnation in Jesus. We are meant to live like Jesus Christ in his divinity and humanity. Just as he unveiled the divine life of our humanness, we, too, must unveil the divine in our lives. This is a contemplative process.

Contemplation is letting go of our thoughts and our ego as our reality center. We turn to the divine within by letting go of our self as the center of our awareness. We let go of our preoccupation with our ego. It is fasting from all the identities with which we name ourselves so that we can know ourselves as expressions of our Father's love. This is what Jesus learned as he came to know himself as the "beloved child" of the Father.

"You are my Son, the Beloved; with you I am well pleased."
Luke 3:22

I don't want this to sound too dramatic because then it becomes overwhelming and seems impossible; it is really very simple and natural. It is a matter of resting in the silence of God. As Jesus abandoned himself into our humanity we abandon ourselves into his divinity.

Abandon is one of those dramatic and overwhelming words that hides a simple reality. When I was a junior in high school, Father Emmett Collins, C.Ss.R., told me, "You work too hard at praying. It's really very simple. Relax a little." Now, forty years later I'm finally getting his meaning. It *is* simple. It is letting God do the work and take the lead in teaching us to let go. But we are so goal driven, so oriented toward "getting it done" that relaxing feels unnatural. A friend who is in Alcoholic Anonymous has told me repeatedly, "You have to let go and let God."

A Surprise Stocking Stuffer

Resting in God begins by letting go, for just a few moments, of our judgments and thoughts, memories, and sensations. We don't try to grasp God, or understand God, or earn God's love. God is here for us or we wouldn't exist. We can let go because God continues to love us into being.

> *Contemplation is a long, loving look at the Real.*
>
> William McNamara[1]

Amazingly, when we let go, our sense of self is replaced by a new foundation. We feel more real, more truly our selves. A new source of confidence replaces our "self-confidence." This all happens, not by trying to make it happen, but by letting go and trusting in God.

Even if we don't "trust" God, just the intention to rest in God allows God room to teach us to trust and let go. For me, letting go is something that is happening *to* me. It is a gift I receive, not something I do for myself.

The gift comes as a surprise. When I look for it and when I try to let go of myself, I am just putting myself—my ego—back in control. But when I turn to God, I am "let go." It happens *to* me.

It is like that Christmas morning three years ago when I woke up after two weeks of battling the flu. On a crisp winter morning, the rising sun was a soft rose color, unlike the bright reds and oranges of summer and fall. I felt alive again, myself again. The flu had drained my energy and now I felt the gift of energy. It was as if, on this Christmas morning, I realized that the true gift stuffed into my stocking was myself, beautifully wrapped in God's life-giving love. I had not had that joyous a Christmas since I got my bicycle.

Unfortunately, the words we have to point to this possibility of grateful and joyous living all sound so negative. Expressions such as *mortification, self-denial, giving up your life, detachment*, and so on are not meant to designate anything except the freedom we can know by letting go of our ego. Dying is really gaining—the gain of full and total life. This is possible only when we withdraw our "ego activity" far enough to let our real self, the life of God, shine into our being.

> *"If any want to become my followers, let them deny themselves and take up their cross and follow me. For those who want to save their life will lose it, and those who lose their life for my sake will find it."*
>
> MATTHEW 16:24–25

Detachment is just an inner letting go that starts with an intention to trust. It is not something we do, but something we allow God to teach us. When it happens, we feel a new sense of inner freedom. Too often we have approached detachment as an act of mind and will, as something we should make ourselves do because it's a good idea or pleasing to God. But that approach misses the point and just leads to attachment to our will. Detachment leads to God's will, not by trying to do his will, but by surrendering to God's love.

> *Surrender is the simple but profound wisdom of yielding to rather than opposing the flow of life...It is to relinquish inner resistance to what is.*
>
> Eckhart Tolle[2]

Holding onto attachments is like holding onto a cold. They leave us with no appetite, no taste, no energy for anything but the cold. Blurry eyes and a stuffy nose block any possibility of appreciating anything else.

Letting go is the essence. It is a release rather than a striving. It is a trusting that God is here for us, loving us unconditionally, rather than trying to gain God's attention or win favor. It is the deeply personal willingness to trust that God is here for us and to cooperate with God as the center and source of our being.

I once facilitated a discussion group on Anthony de Mello's book *Awareness*. We met at Transitions, a local bookstore. Twenty-four people showed up with dog-eared copies of the book. Many had also watched and listened to his video and audiotapes and had read many of his other books. In *Awareness* he repeatedly tells us to "See through it" (p. 16), "Drop your false ideas" (32), "Wake up!" (27), and "Don't seek the truth, just drop your opinions!" (73).[3] When I mentioned that maybe we should take his advice and just spend some silent time, the group stopped, looked at me as if I had begun speaking in some strange language, and then continued its discussion. Silence, doing nothing, just does not make much sense to our goal-oriented mindset.

This first step is the hardest. We are used to working for what we want. Letting go, letting ourselves accept love, trusting that God is already here with us, this truly is a foreign concept. It takes a leap of faith to begin, or at least a willingness to try.

We Let Go to Make Room for Everything

Incarnation means loving all of what it means to be human, just as God does. God's plan for a redeemed world lies embedded in the human endeavor embraced in all its splendor and fragility. The Incarnation invites us into our human limitations as the holy place where blessing awaits us, invites us into the limits of our being as the place of meeting the unlimited God. There we can learn to depend on God rather than on our inflated ego. Our ego wants us to believe that there are no limits—at least for us. Incarnation teaches us to accept our limits so that we can be aware of our desire for the unlimited Divine.

This is possible because God's love is unconditional. Incarnation reminds us that faith in Jesus actually begins with Jesus' faith in us. Jesus is the primary one who has faith, full awareness, and trust in the Father's love. And then he also has faith "in us" in the sense that he sees us as the children of the Father that we really are. He sees through the tight, fearful, grasping, wounded, and hurting experiences that we have mistakenly identified as our selves.

Jesus continues his Incarnation by drawing us away from our self-absorption so that we can participate in the divine life. In Jesus, we come to know that this unbelievable relationship that the Father has initiated with our human race serves a divine purpose. Our lives are part of something much bigger than ourselves.

> The supreme purpose of God is birth. He will not be content until his Son is born in us. Neither will the soul be content until his Son is born in it.
>
> Meister Eckhart[4]

Our ability to accept this extravagant love often collapses under the pressure of our insecurities. I remember turning to a soon-to-be-bride at her wedding rehearsal, and asked, "Are you wearing a blusher?" "Oh, no," she said, "do I look too red?" I was talking about the short veil many brides wear over their face as they walk down the aisle. I wanted to remind her father to lift it up before he kissed her. We interpret other people's words, as well as God's word, through our insecurities.

The good news that Jesus proclaims in his life and in his person is meant to awaken us to God's immediate, sustaining, embracing, and inclusive power in our lives. This alone will free us to love in a way that makes human life worth living. As we grow to trust God's intimacy, we develop a gentle vision that allows us to lay aside our ego and to grasp the world as it is without the defensive judgments created to compensate for the illusion of a distant God.

The Incarnation and our incarnation are possible because of God's unconditional love. Incarnation is concerned with a new experiencing and grasping of reality. It does not lead out of this world, but into the heart of the moment, into life. It is not about contempt for the world, but an entirely new form of love for it. We are meant to love unconditionally as God loves us.

The Incarnation as a fact of our lives means the Father is here; this is his world and we are his people. His dwelling place is not in some invisible and faraway realm, but in the hearts of his children, his people. Incarnation is the truth of our nature fully known and lived because we can trust God's love.

The Unexpected Gift of the Christmas Season

The Christmas story speaks to both the fragility and resilience of the human and the divine person who we are. December 25 was chosen for this feast as a way of "baptizing" the pagan celebration of the sun king. Now it seems the favor has been returned. The celebration of the God who is so intimately close to us as to become human has been replaced by an unattainable God for whom we substitute a pile of gifts.

Advent is meant to attune us to the unveiling of the incredible closeness of God as the source of our own spiritual being made flesh, but what is revealed is a spiritual void. We are driven in the relentless pursuit of foraging and hunting and gathering gifts. Our religious images are trivialized in a vain effort to find comfort in the sweet image of a cuddly divine child.

As dark as this sounds, it could also be the opportunity for an appreciation of the truth of our incarnation. Christmas teases us into letting our longing for love and yearning for wholeness become conscious and be felt. This yearning is the rest of our story; usually we get by, wrapped in consumption, wound tightly in the urgent matters of work, decorated with our possessions. Christmas unwraps our deeper longing as we begin to feel what we generally try *not* to feel.

When our expectations are inflated and later found to be empty, we are at a graced moment. The possibility of awareness, of seeing through the distortions of our culture into our real longing, is awakened. Our basic human desire to survive and our divine desire to be joyously alive are given the shelf space they need in the economy of our attention.

We have had our chance to provide for ourselves and if it leaves us empty, that means we have space available inside to attend to something other than the self. The power of the gospel images of Christmas is not in aggression but in silent, patient waiting. Their value is not that of a timeless truth or an immutable dogma but of a particular moment, when the divine/human child punctured history in a decisive way.

In the Divine Child love is real to our senses, reaching out in vulnerability to our hearts and guiding us to here and now as the only moment of possibility. The wonder it works is not on an intellectual plane but soaks down into us and nourishes our experience of our selves. It takes that which is wounded about us and accepts it unconditionally as the motivation needed to appreciate our humanness.

The higher our expectations for Christmas, the more we try to control Christmas, and the more we make a mess of it. However, because the human is soaked in the divine, even the mess, gaudiness, and sentimentality become the bearer of the surprise and splendor of God's wild extravagance. We have all sat with anticipation as a child opens our gifts to them, only to watch the child become totally absorbed by the bubble wrap meant to protect the gift. I have friends who watch *National Lampoon's Christmas Vacation* as their preparation for the season. They watch it as a documentary. It deflates their grandiose schemes and brings them down to earth. And strangely enough, earth is the place where we experience the joy for which we were created.

In the midst of frustration and confusion, amid the mundane mutterings of our life, the ever-generous offer of deeper intimacy and full-life engagement with God glistens in the eyes of an infant. A tiny, vulnerable infant brings hope, healing, and life to a broken and dying world. This infant will grow up to be the Redeemer, the Messiah whose triumph is the cross. Who would have ever guessed this possibility? Even more wondrously, this means that every infant shares these possibilities in the limitations of human flesh and blood. Who could have ever guessed this reality?

The Child Wakes Up the Child in Each of Us

The image of the Divine Child in a crib seeps into our awareness. Because our lives feel so precarious and we are so anxiety-driven, we need this gentle, compassionate child to charm us. Even as adults the Child in the crib calls out to the child within each of us.

I was waiting for my plane in the Dallas–Fort Worth airport when a little girl ran by me. She had that stiff-legged stride of a child who is just getting used to being upright. She was intent on something. And then I saw her target—another young child in a stroller. She ran up to about ten feet from him and then stopped; she didn't know exactly what to do next. But she was thoroughly engrossed in this other child.

The child within us responds to children. Who but a child can get us down on the floor, making strange faces and strange noises? And Jesus tells us it is the child within us that will attune us to the kingdom of God: "Truly I tell you, whoever does not receive the kingdom of God as a little child will never enter it" (Luke 18:17).

The Divine Child in the crib gets us to relax our defenses, to be less serious, and to try on the new reality of our identity as children of God. This is where to start for most of us. *Incarnation* is conceptual and abstract. It helps us understand and integrate the experiences freed up by the image of the

Child in the crib. The image softens us and helps us relate to God and to the sacred within us with more openness, with a beginner's mind, with a child's openness.

Concepts usually delude us into believing that we have integrated what we understand. Understanding incarnation as our reality and living it are not the same. The mystery of our incarnation combines the unlimited divine reality and the limits of our time and space within the one reality of our person. To know the meaning of our incarnation, we must learn to accept both our need to become more than we are and our desire to avoid change.

This process begins by approaching ourselves without criticism, judgment, and labels. Notice children at the zoo. They accept each animal with wonder and delight. They do not criticize a giraffe for failing to look like a lion. We, too, need to live with an inner spaciousness that allows room for seeming contradictions.

The Incarnation cannot be reduced to either its divine or human elements. It is always more than a symbol of the divinity that often lies dormant within us. It is also a historical event, but more than an event locked into a historical time and space. It is the Divine reality continuing in our reality.

> ...[H]e has given us, through these things, his precious and very great promises, so that through them you may escape from the corruption that is in the world because of lust, and may become participants of the divine nature.
>
> 2 Peter 1:4

Incarnation is about the concrete, the here and now, as well as the beyond. We do justice to it, not by minimizing the importance of the historical birth of Jesus Christ, but by taking to ourselves, as he did, the mystery of embodying the "divine nature" (2 Peter 1:4). His form of being is our form of being. He is the firstborn of this creation. We are his brothers and sisters.

The power of the Incarnation, as a template and source

of our healing and becoming, is that it establishes love as the concrete foundation for our transformation. We become our true self in learning to love unconditionally with God's love.

God walks among us as one like us. As John's Gospel so graphically tells us, "And the Word became flesh and lived among us, and we have seen his glory, the glory as of a father's only son, full of grace and truth" (John 1:14). The Divine walks among us to manifest the reality and closeness of divine presence. So close, and so real, that the divine outpouring of love is the source of our reality. The Divine walks among us to lead us to our shared reality. This means that when we try to understand ourselves, when we ask "Who am I?" we must more accurately ask, "Whose am I?" We are Divine Love's continued expression.

I am, you are, we are the outpouring of love. We are loved absolutely and unconditionally or we would not exist. Spirituality is about letting this reality permeate every aspect of our being, psyche, understanding, and experience. Spirituality works by letting go, letting ourselves be taught to trust.

This is not something that we do for ourselves. We are brought into this awareness, gently guided and healed by Love. It is not a gap we can ford on our own. This is why Love manifests itself in the Word become flesh. God identifies with our humanness as the only way we can be healed and brought to our wholeness. Flesh and blood, here and now, is where God works with us. Only by being as human as we can be are we able to be truly and fully like our brother, Jesus. In opening up to the vulnerability of being human, we find the divine alive within us.

Who We Are Because of Who Jesus Is

If the image of the Divine Child in the crib, if the mystery of Incarnation as our own reality, is going to impact our lives, then it must affect the way we imagine ourselves. It must reform our identity, the reality we identify as being us. This in turn will change the way we imagine our relationship with God and one another.

This is by no means a simple task. The type of change involved is not simply a change of ideas—I exchange my old idea of who Jesus, and God, and I are and form a new idea. It is a different way of experiencing Jesus, God, and myself. It reaches through our mind, past our emotions and memories, into our true self, that place where our loving Creator holds us in existence by pouring out the divine self as our life.

Funerals often plunge us into this deep inner place. They barrage us with emotions that bewilder our mind's attempt to feel in control. And they face us with the ultimate questions about who we are, who God is, and what exists beyond our sensory awareness.

My Aunt Mary died recently. She was ninety-eight. She lived most of her life in David City, Nebraska. Her husband, Frank, was the local blacksmith. He died ten years ago. Aunt Mary spent her last years in Saint Joseph's Villa, where she was well cared for. But this tells you nothing of who she was.

A few intriguing details of her life give you a little more feeling for who she was. Forty years ago a close friend told her that pizza tasted terrible. Mary carried that belief into eternity. She was usually a positive and supportive person. But whenever pizza was mentioned (Pizza Hut is one of three places to get a meal in David City), she would wrinkle her nose and say, "Helen told me that's no good."

Another detail, and this was a surprise to me, was that she was married before she married my Uncle Frank. Her first husband disappeared soon after their wedding. Speculation is that he was part of the Omaha Mob and the charred remains of his body were found in the burning rubble of an abandoned country school. Nobody knows for sure. But it doesn't fit my image of this kind, gentle woman who thought watching the soaps was living on the edge.

I heard many stories at Mary's wake. But one thing surfaced over and over: Mary Straka loved deeply, consistently, and constantly. That's how we, her family, knew her. And it was so good to hear this affirmed by people who lived with her and took care of her. There were even two high-school girls who attended the wake and funeral because they had felt her love. Now you know something real about my aunt.

A funeral faces us with reality. First, the reality of the person who has died, but also our own reality. It stops all our schemes for the future. It is beyond our control. It happens and we have to deal with it, no matter what appointments are on our calendar. It leaves us vulnerable. Our senses cannot perceive the reality of what our faith tells us. And our minds cannot generate ideas to encompass it. Death just is. And it is before us, in our face, exposing our own vulnerability and insecurity.

Paradoxically, this can be a graced moment, just as shattered Christmas expectations can let new light into our world. When we lose our illusion of control, something more real and true can break into our awareness. We can begin to sense the eternal and divine dimension of ourselves.

A lot of conversation around a funeral is an attempt to regain some kind of control by trying to make sense out of what is happening. The night after my aunt's funeral, my youngest sister Kathy, my niece Jennifer, and I stayed up talking. We talked about many things, and of course, God and heaven and hell and what happens in death were major topics. I mentioned my sense of God as the source of our being, that we are an outpouring of God's love, held in existence at every moment by love. And because God's love is faithful and eternal, we are eternal.

Very softly, Jennifer said, "I feel like I want to cry. I've never heard this before." And I felt so good. Jennifer had gotten it. She had been touched by the immediacy and immensity of God's love for her. So, Jenny, I hope you are still feeling this. It is your birthright as a divine and "beloved" child of God.

But it is also going to be hard to believe. There isn't much unconditional love in our world. We have been brought up with an image of a distant God whose love we win by obedience. This is how we have learned to make sense of our reality. To let go of it is to let go of what seemed certain and clear and understandable. To let go of it means we have to find other reasons and motivations to do the good things that we have been taught that God demands. To let go of it means we must find an experiential rather than just an intellectual foundation for our identity.

Our Mind Gets in the Way

From experience I find that letting go of negative images of God who judges and punishes and who wants to bend us to his will is just the beginning of finding a way to open my heart to God. I have no doubt that God loves me unconditionally. My life, my reading, my understanding of Scripture have brought me to this belief. However, believing is not the same as knowing. My beliefs are comforting, but something is preventing them from connecting me to the life-giving experience of God's presence.

> Our heart yearns in simple, silent pleading for action that does not mimic love but springs forth from it.
>
> Gerald May[5]

I am fortunate to live with a Redemptorist community and a parish community that are genuine, generous, and sincere with their support. I receive a great deal of encouragement, and I have tried to support others and affirm their gifts. Somehow this doesn't reach deep enough. It creates a warm glow but not much more.

Sometimes in the dark, quiet hours of the night I wake up feeling possessed by worries swirling around in my head.

At times I can grab hold of a worry and know that I have handled this situation in the past. It is really nothing to worry about. But my mind is off, chasing down another worry. Why do I conjure up these negative scenarios? Except that my mind seems to delight in imagining them. It's like my mind is tormenting me.

I have also noticed that when I'm angry at someone I create a story of how they've offended me and images of just how vile they are. When I want to elicit sympathy or support from friends, I replay the drama in my head so that I can share what I'm feeling and why. Replaying it stirs up the anger, hurt, and resentment. Often the replay and regeneration of all these negative and troubling feelings occurs regardless of whether I want them.

When I'm not replaying these dramas, an ongoing commentary takes place in my head—speculating, judging, comparing, complaining, liking, disliking, and proclaiming my worth at the expense of others. This incessant monologue turns whatever is happening in my life into an urgent problem. This means I must deal with it immediately—except that my mind moves on before I can even begin to focus.

The mind is a superb instrument if we use it correctly, but generally it is using us. And it is the mind that is the barrier to an immediate experience of God present and loving.

Almost all of us suffer from the mistaken belief that we are our minds. We identify so closely with our minds that we don't know any other possibility. We actually have the power to give less attention to these monologues, mental movies, and story loops inside our heads. When we take them less seriously, we feel an immediate relief and sense of peace. But until we become aware that we can let go of our attachment to them, they seem to have a life of their own.

The desire to let go of negative images of God is a first step in consciously connecting to Love as the source of our self. Becoming aware of how our mind works is the necessary second step. Meditation methods and contemplative prayer free us from the dominance of our minds. But the most powerful purgative is a relationship with God's Word, the divine Son who has become flesh and blood as the manifestation of our union with the Father. Who we truly are, who God is, cannot be known conceptually. This is why Jesus draws us into a relationship with God, our Father, and through him into our true self.

Unfortunately, our mind is in the way again. Our image of Jesus has been shaped by our mind into an unattainable abstraction.

A Conspiracy of Humanities: Our Mind

Understanding our mind's tendency to use abstract ideas as substitutes for what really is will help us come closer to knowing Jesus in the fullness of his humanity and divinity. On the one hand, we deny the limits of his concrete humanity. This reduces his life and message to an unattainable ideal, which means that we can try to imitate him, to mimic him, and at the same time absolve ourselves from accepting him as a serious model for our own lives. We can look up to Jesus, we can love him, and we can be challenged by him, but only to a point. According to this image, Jesus is just too much for our failed humanity to accept as a serious possibility for our own lives. We have made him a superhero instead of our brother. We have stressed his divinity without believing in our own.

When I was a kid my favorite TV show was *Superman*. The most thrilling part of the show was to see Superman fly. Every time he soared onto the screen I felt a rush of joy. If my memory holds true, the show began something like this: "Faster than a speeding bullet, more powerful than a locomotive, able to leap tall buildings in a single bound. Look, up in the sky! It's a bird! It's a plane! It's Superman! Strange visitor from another planet, who came to Earth with powers and abilities far beyond those of mortal men, and who, disguised as Clark Kent, mild-mannered reporter for a great metropolitan newspaper, fights a never ending battle for truth, justice and the American Way."

I still thrill at these words. But they're Superman's description, not mine. I can be thrilled by Superman, but I'll never be Superman.

Like Jesus, Clark Kent was a nice guy, not given to boasting, kind and helpful. I knew I could be somewhat like both of these superheroes, a nice kid, kind and helpful. But, of course, both Jesus and Clark had those super powers to rely on when the going got tough. And that's where we parted company. Clark could leap into the air and Jesus could ascend. I was left behind, back here on Earth, a nice guy, but no superhero.

None of us can be a superhero, but it's not enough just to be a nice person, or a "good Christian." Our Father wants us to catch some of his passion and joy. Goodness so easily becomes cheerless and finicky, a technique for working off guilt, devoid of desire, and sterile of love. We so easily become half-alive in a hell of our own creating, poor in spirit and rich in distractions. Many of us become aware of our diminished spirit when we burn out or find ourselves trapped in addiction.

Our Father envisions so much more for his children, "beloved" sisters and brothers of his Son.

> *Beloved, let us love one another, because love is from God; everyone who loves is born of God and knows God. Whoever does not love does not know God, for God is love. God's love was revealed among us in this way: God sent his only Son into the world so that we might live through him. In this is love, not that we loved God but that he loved us and sent his Son to be the atoning sacrifice for our sins. Beloved,*

since God loved us so much, we also ought to love one another. No one has ever seen God; if we love one another, God lives in us, and his love is perfected in us.

By this we know that we abide in him and he in us, because he has given us of his Spirit.

1 JOHN 4:7–13

Our Possibilities Are Divine

"...[I]f we love one another...his love is perfected in us.... By this we know that we abide in him" (1 John 4:12–16). We know who we truly are as divine/human beings when we love, and in loving, we come to know who God is. We can love because the Father and the Spirit continue to create and guide us through loving. Like Jesus we are bound up in the giving and receiving of love, which is the Trinity. This is who we are. This is our true identity. Notice, it is not built around qualities and concepts, but is an expression in our flesh and blood of being loved and being loving.

Jesus' teachings are indivisibly a comment on his life and our own, earthed in his story. They are an expression of his inner self as he comes to know it in his outer experience. It is not like he is acting out a script crafted by his Father. He is commenting on his true self as it becomes manifest in his living. As he tells us what he is about, the implication is that we are about the same thing. We understand the meaning of the Word and his words as we come to understand the meaning of ourselves as his continued expression.

When I catch myself doubting the possibility of loving like this, I think of parents of newborns. When my brother Bob and his wife, Sue, had their first daughter, Caressa, we went out to dinner to celebrate her baptism. Every fifteen minutes Bob and Sue took turns calling the babysitter. They were engulfed by love for Caressa.

I have never been a parent, but as a priest I have known moments when a deep well of love opens up within me. It happens when people are courageous enough to share their hurt and confusion and drop the pretensions of being in control. Their honesty and vulnerability is a divine gift that opens up the immediacy of God's love working between us. At those moments I know how easy it is for God to love us.

The word is made flesh in Jesus by an emergence from within the heart of the Creator. Divinity exists as integral to his human being and living. It was not apparent to his followers in any recognizable way. They were intrigued by him and hoped in him. Most grew to truly love him. But it was not until his resurrection and the subsequent sending of his Spirit that they began to get a glimpse of the fullness of his nature, and theirs.

When we understand that Jesus really was like us, we begin to see that the only process of self-improvement that works is one that does not reject who we are and must begin with all of who we are. It is not about fixing ourselves. It is about being loved and learning to love all of who we are. It is about loving our divine possibilities as well as our wounded and limited humanity. God is already loving us into existence; our part is learning to become aware of and love all of who God loves. Knowing the extent to which Jesus became human helps us accept our humanness.

Jesus experienced apprehension, fear, grief, need, and frustration, and in this came to know the deepest human paradox, that surrender to God leads to resurrection and to transformation as our ultimate meaning.

He asks the woman at the well for water because he is thirsty and weeps for Lazarus because he is stricken with grief. He is frustrated with the dullness of his disciples and angered by the hypocrisy of the religious leaders. At the same time, he is filled with compassion for the sick and the sinful, and begs to be spared his own horror on the cross.

This is his nature—at once fully human and fully divine. His humanity is not a disguise covering the truer reality of his divinity. He is one of us, and the more we understand our deepest nature, the more we'll know him for who he is.

If we learn to appreciate his humanity, we will be able to see in him the qualities that are possible in our own humanness. We can learn from his self-reflection to penetrate our own true self. We will face in ourselves the incredible mystery that Jesus manifests: it is only by becoming divine that we become fully human and only by being fully human that we become divine. To be fully human, to be whole, means that we become aware of all that we are and accept all of who we are.

We exist in the tension between the divine and human poles of our nature. If we affirm one without the other, we collapse either into self-righteousness or self-loathing. We either inflate our ego or deflate our sacred spirit.

My mind wanders to an image from my high school days, and you may remember it in your own high school psychology book—the optical illusion of a woman who was either young and beautiful, or ancient, ragged, and cursed with a wart on her nose, depending on how you looked at her. Our task as sisters and brothers of Jesus is to learn to love both images at the same time. Both are our truth: we are divine and human, sacred and earthy. We need to love ourselves for all of who we are.

Human and Divine: Learning to Be All of Who We Already Are

The best way to expand our image of who we are—to accept what it means to be both divine and limited at the same time—is to cultivate humility. *Humus, human, humor,* and *humility* all come from the same root. We cultivate the earthiness, the humus of our being when we accept our limits, our sensuality, our physicality, and our woundedness, as necessary aspects of being divine flesh and blood. The irony is that without the divine we would probably never notice the rest of our selves.

Humility is simply accepting ourselves for who we are and being willing to see ourselves for all of who we are. It is a respect for ourselves as we are, and a reluctance to force ourselves into the abstract expectations of our ego. Humility is the never-ending adventure of coming to know all the facets of our self, seeing ourselves clearly, and learning to be at home with all of this.

When we pay attention to our whole self we know ourselves as limited, flawed, paradoxical, and imperfect as well as gifted with divinity. We are uncertain yet long for certainty, limited and wounded, yet we crave wholeness. The paradox created by our human and divine nature is what drives us to seek salvation because it leaves us with a haunting sense of incompleteness, of being somehow unfinished. Our only hope is to resist rejecting our self by attempting to deny this paradox. To be complete we need to be humble.

At one time in my life, humility seemed like an affront to my sense of self. It seemed like an attack on my tender sense of self-worth. I fought it by ignoring all the parts of me that did not fit into a positive self-image or that seemed contrary to my sincerely chosen set of personal values and value. This was the only way I could imagine building sorely needed "self" confidence. It did not work well because the parts of myself that I ignored lurked in the dark corners of my awareness like a dark presence against which I guarded myself.

> *Humility is just as much the opposite of self-abasement as it is of self-exultation. To be humble is not to make comparisons. Secure in its reality, the self is neither better nor worse, bigger nor smaller than anything else in the universe. It is nothing, yet at the same time one with everything.*
>
> Dag Hammarskjold[6]

Even my first steps toward recognizing the value, necessity, and openness of humility were mostly pragmatic and negative. I felt that I might just as well admit what everyone else already knew about me. Humility came when I realized God was for me in a way that I could not be for myself.

Humility is accepting the wholeness of our being, trusting in God's guidance. We must learn to accept our divine origin and vocation as well as commit to facing the doubts, limitations, and self-contradictions buried like land mines along the inner path of spiritual development. This is a choice on our part, but it relies on God's graciousness, God's gift of unconditional love.

As I continue contemplative practice I find myself less able to relax and let God be my center. I feel less able to meditate than I could at the beginning. All I can do is be quiet and turn my attention inward. Moments of peace and quiet come as a gift from beyond me; they happen to me. I cannot grasp them for myself. At the same time, I am much more aware of the judgments and self-centered grousing that seems to be my constant companion. I trust that this is the way God is healing me and teaching me to let go. What once was negative and self-deprecating has become a gift of humble trust in God's guidance.

Powerless and Persistent

As humility takes root in our awareness, we come to know our powerlessness and the patient persistence of God's love. We experience ourselves as fragile and resilient beyond all our expectations.

Nothing is more humbling than recognizing and accepting that we are loved without question, without needing to fit an

> The quest does not bring about improvement or perfection.
> It brings about a maturity, a humanity, and a wisdom.
>
> A. H. Almaas[7]

agenda, without cause; we are loved just because we are and because God is God.

We are not loved for any qualities on which our ego stakes its claim. Our mind simply cannot wrap ideas around what our spirit knows. Humility is not about thinking less of our self but rather of gaining a true understanding and awareness of who and what we really are.

Humility is the opposite of pride. Humility loves who we are; pride seeks to aggrandize the self so that it is worthy of love. Humility knows that we are part of something bigger than ourselves. Pride wrestles with reality to subdue it to our needs.

Pride fearfully defends itself. Humility yields to the flow of life as it is. Pride isolates and separates us from one another. Humility surrenders its judgment by letting go of the abstract qualities we pretend to be our strengths. Humility frees us to be compassionate, to connect with one another in our shared humanness.

> The ultimate goal is not communion with God but incarnation, making spirit flesh. Union with God is the first step, the necessary precondition for bringing God to the world.
>
> John Shea[8]

Humility refocuses our life, removing self from the equation that defines the meaning of our life. Humility is about getting out of the way: getting out of God's way and getting out of our own way.

Humility allows us to be at home in the human race, to be at ease with ourselves and one another. Here is something you might not expect: to be divine is to be humble. To be divine is to love humanity so much that we live within its limits. Jesus could not be the Word, the concrete expression of divine love and creativity in time and space if it were not for humanity. Our strengths separate us while our limits and needs unite us.

Humanity is created as the vessel of divine expression.

Humanity is the part of creation that can become conscious of its origins of love and choose to love in return. The word would not have been heard unless there were human ears. The recognition of our earthy nature leads us to affirm that our fundamental nature is dependence. And the word blesses this dependence with the gift of interdependence. Because God wanted to speak, we exist.

And yet the truth of this relationship is like that of a child giving its parents a Christmas gift that the parents paid for. Our intention, our free choice is the gift we bring, and even that is God's gift.

God's But Not Gods

Gifts come from someone else. We cannot give our self a gift any more than we can tickle ourself. Gifts remind us that we are dependent on others and that means that we are not gods and so we cannot be expected to perform as gods. This is a blow to our ego, which would love to demand greater pleasure, freedom without responsibility, total power, and to be held in esteem by all, while denying our human limitations with their vulnerability, physical weakness, and the necessity of work.

> The more we need God the more we feel a need to be god.
>
> John Kirvan[9]

The first thrust of humility is to implant within us an acceptance that we are of the earth and it is pride that makes us expect too much of ourselves.

The more we develop the clarity of vision that is humble honesty, the more we become aware of our mind obstructing our vision, the more we come to understand that we all struggle with the same demons, the same fears and sorrows, the more we will be able to relate to one another with compassion.

We all hope for fulfillment of our desires and happiness and to trust that we are all doing the best with what we have. It is a blessed relief to be at ease with ourselves and one another, and is even more blessed when we can let go of our judgments and bond with one another as compassionate companions discovering the human and divine mystery of our living.

Our True Identity Revealed

"Somewhere Over the Rainbow" is playing on my CD player as I write this. Images of bluebirds flying over the rainbow touch me in that place where I am being created at this moment. It is a childlike place—a place of hope and earnest longing, a place where I have learned to trust a God whose love I cannot feel and whose necessity I cannot ignore, a place where heaven and earth mix.

The image of the Child in the crib speaks directly to that same place in all our hearts. The Child in the crib as a vulnerable child allows us to be vulnerable to our own deep need and divine penchant for love.

I was in eighth grade when my youngest sister, Kathy, was born. I vividly remember holding her while she slept, feeling her heart beat and listening to her breathing. She was so peaceful, so trusting, so delicate, and exquisitely beautiful. I remember feeling so proud that she trusted me and at the same time feeling a fierce need to protect her with my life. I don't know if I was just being dramatic. Those were not my usual feelings in eighth grade.

Babies do that to us. They get through to us. At the supermarket yesterday a young man held a baby. The man's head was shaved bald and his arms were tattooed. Muscles rippled under his T-shirt and tender pride glowed in his eyes. I don't know why he needed to be so tough, but the baby let him be tender, proud, and loving. That's the power of the divine/human Child in the crib: he speaks directly to our hearts.

The Christmas season allows us to hope in our illusions and discover that they cannot satisfy our deepest need. With this comes the revelation that the loving God we encounter in the Child in the crib is present in our need for love and as the meaning of our desires.

The innocence of this image is its power. This baby is the God upon whom Moses and the prophets could not look and live, the word of God spoken to Job from the whirlwind and the Spirit, brooding over the waters of chaos at the beginning of creation, is among us as a newborn. The God, the divine and unlimited pure spirit, whose only adequate expression is silence, is spoken as the "Word."

> In the beginning was the Word, and the Word was with God, and the Word was God. He was in the beginning with God. All things came into being through him, and without him not one thing came into being.
>
> John 1:1–3

The Divine Child gives us an image of our own human divinity and identity. This Child reaches out from the heart of love to offer love as our own identity. If we want to know love as our own deepest identity, we begin by remembering that we are loved beyond all imagining, or we would not exist. Like the Child in the crib we burst forth from the heart of God, whose creative essence is love. Love is the essence of our spirit. To the extent that we experience this and allow it to saturate our awareness, we will also be loving.

Imagine that every atom, every molecule, every grain of sand, every rock, every mountain, every living thing, every beam of light, every bit of your self, *everything*, is bursting forth, cascading radiant love, showering every other bursting forth of love. We exist at this moment because we are passionately loved into existence.

All of this is revealed in the humanity of Jesus, precisely in his thirst, his common lot with us, his desire to avoid the cross (and if it is not possible, his acceptance of its necessity), his compassion for our shared suffering, and his willingness to enter into forgiveness with us.

This is how God saves, by becoming dependent, fragile, powerless, one of us. We are talking about the birth of a child, not the conquering armies of a powerful man or the scientific breakthrough of a genius or the pious actions of a saint. This is an act of deepest intimacy that appeals to the common instincts of the human heart, the desire to survive, be loved and loving, and in all of this know the joy of living in the fullness of our divine/human self. God saves by being with us in the events of living and dying that we are powerless to avoid.

How does one seek union with God? The harder you seek, the more distance you create between Him and you. So what does one do about the distance? Understand that it isn't there. Does this mean that God and I are one? Not one. Not two. How is this possible? The sun and its light, the ocean and the wave, the singer and the song—not one, not two.

Anthony DeMello[10]

We begin to trust our Father's love for us by learning to humbly accept ourselves for all of who we are. This acceptance attunes us to the gift of love happening within us. Whenever we notice a failure to accept ourselves, we ask for the gift to accept that failure as part of "all of who we are." In this school of love, where Jesus is our mentor, we come to realize that God's love for us is integral to our love for others and our innate love for God.

Who We Are Because of Who God Is: The Spirituality of the Child in the Crib

Who are we?

We are the ones who must learn to live a double destiny—human and divine—and who must learn to love all of who we are. This is the only way that we can truly affect the quality of our living and loving. We are the beloved children of God, brothers and sisters of Jesus. We are the ones to whom our silent Father has spoken his word to awaken us to the immediate, sustaining, embracing, and inclusive intimacy of his love.

We are humans, limited by time and space, wounded by fear, anger, and defensive judgments, whom Jesus seeks to heal and the Spirit seeks to transform into a fully free and creative response to divine love. We are the beloved children, the love of the Trinity bursting forth into time and space, who come to know the life, death, and resurrection of Jesus, our brother, as the meaning and healing of our own lives.

We are the ones who, freed by humility, are willing to let go of our ego and mind as the arbiter of value and the locus of control, and thus able to find the spaciousness to let the divine/human mystery of Jesus illuminate our identity.

We are the children with beginner's minds who respond to the human, vulnerable, and divine Child in the crib. This vulnerability frees our own vulnerability so that we can respond from our true self.

We are the ones who are so loved by the Creator of the universe that the Creator becomes one of us and saves us by the intimacy of being with us as our eternal source.

We are the ones whose desires drive us into a consumer stampede every Christmas until we succumb to exhaustion and begin to feel our deepest desire which, joy of joys, is just the mirror image of God's desire for us.

And this is just the beginning of coming to know "who we are because of who God is." Along with Jesus our task is to embody the divine mystery. In the next chapter we will come to know the fierce loyalty and enduring love of our Father as the necessary antidote to our rigid defenses and destructive fear.

chapter 3

The Cross:
God's Heart Laid Bare

John the Evangelist tells us:

"For God so loved the world that he gave his only Son, so that everyone who believes in him may not perish but may have eternal life."

JOHN 3:16

*A*six-foot crucifix hangs on the second-floor landing of Saint Michael's rectory. The first time my four-year-old niece Caressa saw it, she stopped dead in her tracks. "Is Jesus killed?" she asked. For her the crucifix that I have passed so many times without a glance was very real.

When I was first ordained I spent a summer at the "Rock" Church in St. Louis, Missouri. That rectory also has a life-

> We must not concentrate so much on what Christ has done for us and suffered for us, as on the love with which He did it all.
>
> Saint Alphonsus Liguori[1]

sized crucifix on the second-floor landing. Father Joe Fagen, C.Ss.R., was living there at the time. He was an incredibly kind and gentle man, so much so that he spent hours every day hearing confessions. Going to him was like getting a big bear hug from God.

Every evening as we walked from the first-floor dining room to the living room on the second floor, Father Joe would pause to kiss the feet of the crucifix. Like my niece, Christ was very real to him. But instead of terror, Father Joe knew great love and loved greatly.

Today I'm thankful that I had the privilege of living with Father Joe. Faith is caught from people of faith. Now, thirty years later, whenever I pass by the crucifix on Saint Michael's second-floor landing, I pause to remember the great love embodied for us in Jesus. And I thank God that a little of Father Joe's faith caught hold in me.

Saint Alphonsus was very much aware that faith happens through contact with people of faith; this is the reason for much of his writing. He wanted to hand on his faith and his burning awareness of God's love. His advice is deceptively simple, "consider the immense love which Jesus Christ has shown us in his life and especially in his death." He wanted us to move beyond believing that God loves us to actually experience the revelation of God's love. Revelation touches the deepest part of us, bringing healing and the freedom to be loving.

I would like to follow Alphonsus' lead and consider "the immense love" that God our Father and his Son Jesus are for us. The cross of Christ distills the intensity of that loving into a searing light that reveals both the wound that is the cause of violence and the vulnerability that needs to be loved into healing. Hopefully this chapter will provide a chance to pause and consider this "immense love" so that we might catch the inner healing and transformation that Jesus brings to us through his living, dying, and rising.

God's Response to the Scandal of Human Suffering

If you have ever driven on a winding mountain road, you know that every turn reveals new vistas. Every vista revels in a new panorama of beauty. Something about this beauty is both awe-inspiring and hope-inspiring. Something about this beauty makes your feel ennobled and humbled at the same time. As you drive around curve after curve, each reveals its distinctive beauty and elicits your reverence at the splendor of the mountain.

I experience the cross of Christ in much the same way. Every new awareness in my life opens up new vistas. Some are very harsh as they reveal the violence of nature and human nature. Others take my breath away with the overwhelming panorama of the Father's passionate love and the Son's compassionate love for us.

If you have ever, in the elation of the moment, tried to take pictures and capture a mountain's rugged presence and exalted beauty, you know how deflating the results are. Each turn of the mountain road exposes new surprises, while the pictures are flat and trivial in comparison. My hope is that my reflections will encourage you to look for yourself and discover the grandeur of the Father and Son's love for you.

I begin by sharing some of the peaks and valleys that I have happened upon in reading and reflecting on Christ's passion, death, and resurrection. This path has many twists and turns, each eliciting new reverence in response to Christ's love. Yet, as I write them, they seem like snapshots in comparison to "...the immense love which Jesus Christ has shown us in his life and especially in his death." In the end, an appreciation for Jesus' love comes alive only through our own experience, our own relationship to the Son and Father. I hope that the wonders I point to will help in your own relationship.

Christ on the cross is the response of God to the scandal of human suffering. God calls to our heart with deep tenderness, knowing that we are exhausted trying to be our own god. God calls in the Word who lives with our poverty and powerlessness, sharing our vulnerability. God calls us with the Word who is all that we are and love for all that we are.

Jesus' role is far more than a teacher or a good example, or even a moral guide. It is more intimate. Jesus is God with us in every possible way, and his human existence incarnates God's love for us as human beings. In Jesus, the Father's passionate love for all creation becomes flesh and blood in the divine Son whose preaching is a commentary on our possibilities and whose living, dying, and rising is a revelation of all that we can become. We are human and divine and meant to continue Jesus' manifestation of our Father's passionate love. Jesus means to awaken us to our true identity in God, which is beyond the confines of our ego-mind. This means that his cross is not a substitute for our suffering, but an awakening to our true identity in the Father.

> "...[M]ay all be one. As you, Father, are in me and I am in you, may they also be in us, so that the world may believe that you have sent me. The glory that you have given me I have given them, so that they may be one, as we are one."
>
> John 17:20–22

God's Heart Revealed

When we look upon the cross we see God's heart laid open for us. On the cross we see God's compassion and determination to meet us where we are, love us for who we are, and open us to healing and wholeness.

The cross is not a proof of God's love but a consequence of God's love and of the wound that all humans bear. The cross is the salve, the healing balm that goes directly to the source of that wound.

The essence of the wound that afflicts us all is the illusion and belief that we are separate from God. This illusion makes us look to ourselves as the center of our lives, actions, and security. The fact is, God is the center: God loving us unconditionally and holding us in existence. Whenever, in any way, we forget this, we reopen the wound. That is why so many of our best intentions are destructive or ineffective. They place us once again at the center of our lives. They inflict and reinforce our illusion of separation from God who is love for us.

When I hear confessions I often wait until the person has completed the list of things for which he or she is sorry and then I ask, "Of all these things you've mentioned, which one is the most important to you right now? Which one would you like to have God help you with?" It is a way of trying to help the person connect to God rather than their feelings of guilt.

Very often their answer is "Patience. I want to be more patient with my husband, my wife, my children, and the people I work with." Then I ask, "Have you tried to be more patient?" "Yes" is the answer. "And how has it worked?" I ask. "It works for a little while, but then I find myself getting critical, angry, and impatient again. And now I'm angry and impatient with myself."

We will not overcome impatience by being impatient with ourselves. Trying to change ourselves usually doesn't get very far because we are caught in a spiral of self-destruction.

This is why Saint Alphonsus' simple advice to "...consider the immense love..." is so profound. For these people it would translate into this kind of advice, "Instead of taking this change upon yourself, start with God's patience and love for you. Whenever you catch yourself being impatient, remember God's patient words, 'You are my beloved...' or at the end of the day, think about the times you have been impatient, and again remember God's patient words for you, 'You are my beloved....'" Remembering God's patient love gently and patiently releases the pressure that comes from reliance on our self, our ego-mind, and will. Remembering God's patient love reminds us that God is the center of our lives and to make room for healing. This is our chance for real healing. Healing is far different than changing how we act. We can learn to mimic patience, or we can be healed into peacefulness.

We Exist, Not by Our Own Efforts, but by Our Father's Love

Our ego-mind and will are by their nature critical, judgmental, and impatient. They focus on our limitations and highlight the ways we fall short of ideals—either ideals we set for ourselves or that others set for us. They pit us against our self, trying to overcome our self in order to feel better about our self. We need something more lasting and deeply healing. "Consider the immense love…" This is the only resource that can truly heal us. In the gospels we see Jesus becoming aware of this "immense love" and choosing to integrate it into his life.

When Jesus is baptized in the Jordan by John, these words reveal his identity: "You are my…Beloved; with you I am well pleased" (Mark 1:11). These are the words our parched hearts long to drink in and immerse themselves in. *You are my beloved.* These words are also spoken to all of us. Listen to them for yourself. Let them saturate your whole being, *You are my beloved.* The cross is a torrent of the Father's love pouring into the heart of his "beloved" children through his "beloved Son."

"You are my beloved" was spoken first to Jesus so that his life could give us a voice, a healing touch, so that his life could be the seed of new life planted in our imagination. Jesus is the Word manifesting the Father's words. Jesus makes the Father's presence real and available to our awareness, while at the same time giving flesh and blood to the fullness of our human possibilities.

Knowing that we are beloved is only the beginning. It is like knowing that we have to exercise to improve our health. Knowing is not enough; we have to actually exercise to enjoy its benefits. Once we know we are beloved, we must learn to accept this meaning as our own. Our existence and survival are based on this commitment of our Father rather than our own efforts. Fortunately, we have Jesus to show us how to integrate this gift.

In the story of his baptism, we see that Jesus also had to integrate the reality of his Father's love into his adult consciousness. This story continues the account of his baptism with this enigmatic statement, "And the Spirit immediately drove him out into the wilderness. He was in the wilderness forty days, tempted by Satan" (Mark 1:12, 13).

In the Incarnation of Jesus, God's commitment has been to love us and work with us within the limits of our humanness. Jesus gave this commitment flesh and blood, accepting its limits, with all its consequences and learning to rely on God as priority and source of his existence, just as we need to do.

The Spirit leads Jesus into the desert to face the illusion of separateness from God. Satan's method is to use Jesus' basic instincts for survival, power, and esteem as a wedge between Jesus and his Father. Much the same thing happens in our consciousness as it begins to individuate and we lose the security of being identified with the people and environment around us. This perceived diminishing response to our instinctual needs creates fear and anxiety within us. We grasp for anything and any way of meeting these needs. It's like someone who can't swim suddenly in water over their head. They thrash and flail, hoping to grasp anything that will help them survive.

Each of us has gone through this transition. Each of us has grabbed onto something as our way of surviving. As infants we learned ways to manipulate our environment and get our needs partially met. This happened on an instinctual and emotional level of our psyche, before we had developed self-awareness or the use of our rational mind. Later we used our mind to construct an elaborate structure of concepts around this basic method of survival. We identify these concepts as "me." Unfortunately, in doing this our consciousness is focused on the intellectual construct and loses any sense of being connected to our true source, which is God. Even if we do hear the words "You are my beloved," they become just another abstract concept among all the others.

In the desert Jesus confronts this structure of consciousness. At his baptism he became aware of the true source of his identity, the Father's love. And now he must make a choice about which identity he will trust—the ego identity that has gotten him this far or the deeper identity based in love.

The first temptation is subtle, "If you are the Son of God, command this stone to become a loaf of bread" (Luke 4:3). In other words, if you want to survive, take the power into your own hands. And Jesus responds, "One does not live by bread alone" (4:4). My Father remains first in my life.

The second temptation is to buy into the illusion of power and control. Jesus' response is "Worship the Lord your God, and serve only him" (Luke 4:8). Again Jesus remains centered on the Father as the source of his security. He will not try to be his own power.

The most insidious temptation is saved for last: If you believe God loves you so much and protects you, then jump off the tower of the temple, and let God's angels catch you.

Satan is daring Jesus to prove his faith by testing his Father's love. If the Father really values you, Satan insinuates, he would not allow you to be harmed. After all, you are his "beloved."

Jesus' response, "Do not put the Lord your God to the test" (Matthew 4:7). Do not try to turn God into an object, an idol, a magic amulet, whose place is to spare us from the limits of our humanness. God does not serve our ego and God's love cannot be manipulated by our ego.

We Do Not Have to Be God

The good news here is that we are not God, nor do we have to be. The bad news, because of our illusion of being separate, is that to find this out, we have to let go of our desire to protect ourselves by taking God's place in our own lives. Since this desire to be our own source of power and action is created in response to feeling separated, in response to the terrors of feeling on our own, in an attempt to protect our vulnerability, letting go of this desire can be terrifying.

This desire to be a separate and self-protected self is also deeply rooted in our biological instinct for survival. It also is developmentally built into the way our minds function as we try to create our sense of independence. As our brain develops, we become painfully and anxiously aware of our fragility in an overwhelming world. I can remember when a thunderstorm would send me shuddering under my blankets. This natural coming to awareness is further intensified in families affected by excessive stress or violence.

We feel painfully weak, vulnerable, and overwhelmed by the world around us. We feel the truth of our essence, that without God we are terribly fragile. And we grasp for anything that will make us feel safe, appreciated, and in control of our situation.

In this consciousness we judge everything in our experience according to whether it is good or bad for me as a separate individual. Now that we have learned to see ourselves as separate, we are no longer part of a larger whole. We have reduced ourselves to the images we have in our mind and see ourselves as one small person, deficient and alone in a big, scary universe. This makes us even more dependent on protecting and defending these self-images. And the intensity of our defensiveness makes us dangerous to anyone who gets in our way. We experience others as objects who need to be controlled and manipulated so that we can support and protect this image. This is the wound we bear, the source of evil and violence in our world.

The sad thing is that this identification, this self-image, intensifies the illusion of separation from God and that is why it wounds us. When we forget our source in God, we instinctively work to maintain and reinforce our self-image. We begin to believe that this is all the self-being we have and if we don't tend to its welfare, we will be diminished or even destroyed. This makes us defensive and judgmental because our sense of security is attached to these descriptions, these things that can be said about us in comparison to others. Anything that detracts from this feels like it lessens us and leaves us vulnerable.

We all share this same wound, this illusion that we are separated from God and that we must create our own protection. Illusion though it may be, it leaves an empty and insatiable ache in the pit of our consciousness. We feel that we are abandoned to ourselves and feel our humanness, our finitude, and our limitations as a vulnerability that we must protect. To compensate we try to become our own gods.

The Cross: Our Wound Laid Bare

We have invested in a defensive desire to be as God and are well aware of the stinging humiliation of not being good enough, of being inferior, out of control, a failure in regard to our self-imposed expectations. This pain leads us back into a self-destructive cycle. We try to bolster our image by proudly upholding ourselves and diminishing those we oppose.

The cross of Christ confronts this destructive cycle with an image of a man of love, healing, and compassion who is left bleeding and dying. Here is the helpless one. Here is everything that we want to avoid in ourselves: brokenness, poverty, failure, shame. And everything we cling to for safety is shown to be impotent. Worst of all, we are told that this is how we are redeemed, freed to be our best self. Here is where we are saved from the wound inflicted on us. Here is where everything we cling to for strength is shown to be useless and ineffectual.

The cross also confronts us with the consequences of our wound. Do we judge ourselves and others? Here is the one for whom judgment leads to death. Do we reject him? Here is rejection of both the Son and the Father. Do we seek power? Well, here is what power does to the loving one and here is where weakness triumphs.

What I want to suggest—as we look into the heart and compassion of Jesus, who is the fullest expression of our Father—is that anything that adds to the illusion of separation plays on our most self-destructive anxieties.

> God's love was revealed among us in this way: God sent his only Son into the world so that we might live through him. In this is love, not that we loved God but that he loved us and sent his Son to be the atoning sacrifice for our sins.
> 1 John 4:9–10

The source of evil is a form of "seeking to preserve one's life" because we believe the lie that "if I don't seek to preserve it, it won't be preserved." This is the "father of lies," the falsehood on which all sin is based. Redemption and salvation, therefore, is not a matter of appeasing God. What needs "appeasing" is the craving for security that blinds us to our Father's loving presence. The things we have labeled as "sins" are just symptoms of this deeper wound. Only intimate love can cast out the destructive fear in our wounded human hearts. Being loved is the only thing powerful enough to take the place of our desire to be our own protector.

The Cross Is Not About Suffering to Pay God Back

How does the crucifixion of Jesus save and redeem us? The answer we are accustomed to hearing is that Jesus is a sacrifice to appease God's justifiable wrath. However, sacrifice, as a way of appeasing God's wrath or gaining God's favor, is a pagan notion. In the Christian testament, it is the Father and Son who sacrifice themselves because of their love for us. The Father of Love has no need to be appeased, nor is wrath aimed at our wound justifiable. It was not a conscious choice on our part, and punishing us will not make it go away.

The cross is much more than a price paid for redemption. God does not impose suffering and pain. The fact that the gospel accounts of Jesus' crucifixion do not emphasize deliverance from suffering as the most important event does not mean that suffering can somehow be justified and ceases to be thoroughly evil.

The gospels are very clear in recognizing pain and suffering as evil. Suffering is not imposed as a punishment of sins or the healing of our wound. If this were true, our prisons would be full of saints.

Neither is Jesus' suffering seen as good because it purges and purifies and thus builds character. Even though these happen when some people suffer, what would be the point with Jesus? Suffering is evil, and this is as true for the crucifixion as it is in the instances of blindness and madness that Jesus healed. Redemption is the removal of evil through healing the wound that is its cause.

God does not demand a price for redemption; rather love remains unconditionally present even in the face of the destructive fear that is the source of sin. This is the only way the wound can be healed. Unconditional solidarity creates the freedom that is necessary for love to heal and thrive. Jesus is love committed unconditionally to us in every aspect of our humanness. God is love committed to us in every aspect of our woundedness.

God draws our wounded human heart into his own heart. God does not remove the suffering, does not explain it, nor does he justify it but incorporates it into the mystery of Trinity. The Creator who loves us into being, the Word who reveals that love is the very core of ourselves, the Spirit who is the courage to give that love freely and creatively, now reveal every crisis as received into the mystery of divinity. Healing happens by letting go of our lives and letting God be our life.

Like all of us, Jesus grew in relationship to other humans, and to God, who he came to know intimately as "Father" and who called him "Beloved" (see Luke 3:22). It is this intimate relationship that Jesus brings to us. "Father" expresses our intimacy also. It is how Jesus taught us to address God in our prayer (see Matthew 6:9).

In knowing that we are loved unconditionally, we can look to our Father, rather than power, prestige, and success, as the source of our self. This is salvation, the redemption promised through the Messiah. We no longer live in the illusion of being separate from our true source. The self, which is built around the ego-mind and will with its protective barriers of fear, anger, and isolation, begins to heal.

In learning to be aware as Jesus was aware, we are freed to live from our heart that which is awareness and love created in the "image" of God. When God is first in our lives, everything else finds its proper place.

Love Is Unconditional by Its Nature

By its very nature this kind of love is a response of our whole self, our whole heart, our whole mind, and all our being. It is unconditional. It is giving who we are rather than what we have. We are aware of ourselves as a unity, a whole. This is why loving is so integrating and why it, above everything else, makes us "holy" (whole).

This kind of love is also vulnerable. It is no longer self-protective, angry, and fearful. Its power and authority lie in compassion, nonjudgmental awareness, and generosity. It invites a loving response so that the loved one, "the beloved," can lower their self-protective barriers to give their self to find their heart. It seeks to empower them from their heart. The haunting image of Jesus, so totally vulnerable on the cross, invites the response from inside our heart, our true self. Nothing else is adequate.

In his total opening of himself to God, Jesus became vulnerable, not just to God and goodness, but also to evil. This is the reality of our human situation (see Luke 6:22). And Jesus will not back away.

I believe this leads to a new appreciation of how we grow spiritually. I use "new" in the sense that it is a new perspective, a different way of experiencing, once we come to accept the reality of God's unconditional love and the nature of our wound. It is not new to the many people who have followed the contemplative and mystical path over the centuries.

For those of us, however, who have come from a tradition that emphasizes the separation, reward-and-punishment image of God, it is radically new. It uproots us and grafts us to a new vine, fed by life-giving waters.

Think about the pattern for growing, becoming holy, drawing closer to God, being a better person than we learned as we grew up. Its basic method is this: pay attention to what is wrong with you, decide to change, ask for help and maybe forgiveness from God, and make a firm amendment to change. This approach pits us against our self.

First of all, it asks us to identify our self as the wound rather than know the wound as part of our lives. In this approach, I identify myself as a sinner, I need help, and I must change myself. It puts the burden of change on my shoulders, effectively assigning me to be the center of my life. In other words, it increases the illusion of separation that is the cause of the need for healing in the first place. It asks us to inflict ourselves with the wound and perpetuate the illusion.

This dilemma is poignantly illustrated by this passage in Luke's Gospel (5:17–26):

One day, while he was teaching, Pharisees and teachers of the law were sitting near by (they had come from every village of Galilee and Judea and from Jerusalem); and the power of the Lord was with him to heal. Just then some men came, carrying a paralyzed man on a bed. They were trying to bring him in and lay him before Jesus; but finding no way to bring him in because of the crowd, they went up on the roof and let him down with his bed through the tiles into the middle of the crowd in front of Jesus. When he saw their faith, he said, "Friend, your sins are forgiven you." Then the scribes and the Pharisees began to question, "Who is this who is speaking blasphemies? Who can forgive sins but God alone?" When Jesus perceived their questionings, he answered them, "Why do you raise such questions in your hearts? Which is easier, to say, 'Your sins are forgiven you,' or to say, 'Stand up and walk'? But so that you may know that the Son of Man has authority on earth to forgive sins"—he said to the one who was paralyzed—"I say to you, stand up and take your bed and go to your home." Immediately he stood up before them, took what he had been lying on, and went to his home, glorifying God. Amazement seized all of them, and they glorified God and were filled with awe, saying, "We have seen strange things today."

To let a passage from Scripture do its work of revealing in my life, I start by paying attention to words or phrases that intrigue me: "Jesus perceived their questionings" (he knew their thoughts; Luke 5:22). How many of us are aware of what we're thinking, let alone of what others are thinking? But Jesus knew because he cared. The opposite of love is indifference. Jesus cared and he also knew that their thoughts bound them up in their own pain, he knew how their thinking crippled them and others.

There's a proverb: "When the only tool you have is a hammer, everything looks like a nail." The scribes and Pharisees were critical, vindictive, and judgmental because those were the tools they used to hammer themselves into the narrow confines of their religious practices. Strict adherence to the law and devotional practices had become their way of coping with alienation from God and their own hearts. Therein lies the tragedy—the tools they were using, with the best of intentions, kept them paralyzed and wounded, which made them want to keep the paralyzed man in his place. If there is hope for him, then there is awareness, responsibility, and change for them. That possibility threatens their attempt to feel in control. It shatters their worldview and collapses their defenses, devastating their ego.

This is the tragedy we call *original sin*, the basic wound we all share. When Jesus saw the paralyzed man and the faith of his companions he said, " 'that the Son of Man has authority on earth to forgive sins'—he said to the one who was paralyzed—'I say to you, stand up and take your bed and go to your home' " (Luke 5:24). Faith is trusting God to be the source of our life. Forgiveness means that any barriers that separate us from God and others are gone. In effect, Jesus is telling the paralyzed man, "Know you are healed, nothing stands between you and God." The scribes and Pharisees have faith only in their judgments and laws. These judgments and laws are idols because they take priority over God in their lives.

The image created by this scene is striking. Imagine the scene as an expression of your woundedness and the possibility of its healing. Jesus is in the middle of this small, rustic house. The doorways and windows are jammed with people, and Jesus is surrounded by a circle of scribes and Pharisees, who are seated because they are teachers.

Now, you know that you are crippled, wounded, and cannot continue to live with the deficiency of energy and love that has disabled you. Your faith brings you to Jesus, but you can't approach him directly. With the help of your friends and the courage of their faith, you find a more creative way. When you are lowered down, you find yourself face to face with Jesus, but you are also surrounded by the scribes and Pharisees. They are the part of you that is angry, hurt, and judgmental, and so frightened that it wants to keep you crippled. They are the part of you that wants to keep you away from Jesus, from the summons of love. They are the deafening roar of self-disparaging judgments that keep you from hearing the words of love that you crave. They are all that you have learned throughout your life about making yourself a good and attractive person. They are all the qualities with which you identify and by which you define yourself. They are a reminder that you are a failure—after all, you are crippled.

Jesus had one thing to tell you, "Child you are forgiven. Nothing stands between you and God's love. Except the scribes and Pharisees, that part of you that wants to hold onto the way you do things, and know things, and feel in control. Who are you going to listen to?"

Look into Jesus' eyes to find the connection to God's love and the courage to let go of your paralysis, get up, and walk.

In our heart we meet God's heart exposed, calling us to

let go of our fear and anger and desire to be in control. The cross of Christ radically reframes the way we perceive our lives. It forces us to ask, "what is it that I really want, really desire, really need?"

Could Hell Be the Way to Wholeness?

Our minds build our lives around our needs for success and survival, affection and esteem, power and control. And like the younger son in the parable of the Prodigal Son (see Luke 15:11–32), we separate ourselves and go off to be on our own.

Ross V., a member of Alcoholics Anonymous, once said; "Religion is for those who fear hell. Spirituality is for those who have been there."[2] Maybe like the younger child in the story of the Prodigal Son, we have to live in our separate hell long enough to be ready to seek forgiveness and come back home. A Chinese proverb tells us "The best way to get over sickness is to be sick of it." Maybe once we have had enough of the hell of separation we are ready to find our way back to the Father. The incredibly joyful and good news is, that if we look up, the Father is running down the hill, arms wide open to embrace us, shouting from the top of his lungs for all to hear, "this [child] of mine was dead and is alive again" (Luke 15:24).

Of course, we can also respond like the older child in this story. We have worked hard to be the best that we can be. We have kept our nose to the grindstone. While our younger sibling has lived a life of joyless extravagance, we have lived a life of joyless duty. We have notched up victories over sin and developed well-manicured virtues. We have made our-selves all that we are, become all the qualities that are highly respected. Once we have noticed that being all these things does not make us happy, then our Father in his compassion-ate love can gently point us to true happiness. We begin with the awareness that responsibility for our unhappiness and the possibility for happiness sits squarely on our shoulders: "You are always with me, and all that is mine is yours" (Luke 15:31). What is stopping you from enjoying all that you have?

More importantly, what is stopping us from experiencing the joy and happiness for which we are created? What is stopping us from knowing how intimately, realistically, and passionately we are loved by our Father? What is blinding us and binding us?

The Golden Chain That Blinds and Binds

Throughout the gospels Jesus has an uncanny knack of exposing exactly what it is that binds and blinds us. For the most part, we are blinded and binded by a golden chain. It looks beautiful, valuable, and necessary, but it ties us to our fears and uses these fears to blind us to God's presence. For example, in dealing with the Rich Young Man, we see how Jesus very gently rattles the golden chain. The invitation to freedom and fullness of life must be gentle or it easily becomes a new binding and blinding, using fear and guilt to forge its links.

> *Then someone came to him and said, "Teacher, what good deed must I do to have eternal life?" And he said to him, "Why do you ask me about what is good? There is only one who is good. If you wish to enter into life, keep the commandments." He said to him, "Which ones?" And Jesus said, "You shall not murder; You shall not commit adultery; You shall not steal; You shall not bear false witness; Honor your father and mother; also, You shall love your neighbor as yourself." The young man said to him, "I have kept all these; what do I still lack?" Jesus said to him, "If you wish to be perfect, go, sell your*

*possessions, and give the money to the poor, and you
will have treasure in heaven; then come, follow me."
When the young man heard this word, he went away
grieving, for he had many possessions.*

*Then Jesus said to his disciples, "Truly I tell you,
it will be hard for a rich person to enter the kingdom
of heaven. Again I tell you, it is easier for a camel
to go through the eye of a needle than for someone
who is rich to enter the kingdom of God." When the
disciples heard this, they were greatly astounded and
said, "Then who can be saved?" But Jesus looked at
them and said, "For mortals it is impossible, but for
God all things are possible."*

MATTHEW 19:16–26

Jesus accepts the young man's question as sincere, but
in the face of his claim to have kept all the commandments,
Jesus rattles the young man's golden chain. Jesus' response
exposes the young man to his dependence on his "many possessions."

Frankly, I feel for the young man, probably because I
find this to be true for myself. I am not rich or even young
anymore, but there are things I am attached to and they feel
more important than they are. Although I know that these
attachments are an illusion, I'm still not inclined to let go of
them. And according to the scenario I've heard preached all
my life, until I can reject possessions and give them to the
poor, I cannot proceed along the spiritual path. Fortunately,
Jesus has something more life-giving in mind. "For mortals it
is impossible, but for God all things are possible" (Matthew
19:26). We cannot do it for ourselves, but we can learn to
receive from God's possibilities.

Jesus exposes the young man's golden chain without re-
buke; indeed, no words of his even mention this dependence.
It is simply the suggestion of giving it all up that shows the

young man where his heart lies. It is not a matter of Jesus laying down the law or presenting an ideal quality for attainment or even condemning possessions. In bringing the reality to the young man's awareness, Jesus begins to free him from being possessed. It is a matter of consciousness and love, not mind and will. The invitation to freedom must be just that, an invitation. And it must be gentle, because it is touching a tender and defended spot in the young man's awareness. If it remains a matter of mind and will, it will leave him just as bound to spiritual pride as he had been to possessions.

Chained by Our Limited Identity

The answer to our earlier question, "What is stopping us?" is also exposed in this encounter with the rich young man. "What is stopping us" is our identification with our personal qualities, our strengths ("Teacher, I have kept all these since my youth"; Mark 10:20), favorite assets, and possessions that we feel are necessary to our lives because they create our sense of self. These have become sophisticated survival techniques, our way of getting along in this world, but they no longer serve their original purpose.

We have learned to act friendly or aggressive, enticing or cooperative, realistic and insightful, loyal and caring. We have learned to surround ourselves with possessions and to possess success, all as ways of ensuring our survival and comfort. These are the golden chains that bind us. They dazzle and blind us, even in the light of awareness. They were created as our response to our basic instincts for survival, esteem, and power. They were created when we began to feel separated from the divine source of our life. In fact, they have helped us get to this point in life. But now they have become compulsive behavior patterns, distortions in our perception. They blind us to the intimate and life-giving presence of our Father.

Jesus, and the gospels, strive to heal our blindness and break the bindings of these golden chains. Jesus wants to awaken us to the pure awareness and unconditional love that is our true self, so that we can be joyful, loving participants in creating the Father's kingdom for all people.

I don't want to give you the impression that breaking the golden chain is manageable, doable, just a matter of setting our mind to the task. Awareness and good intentions are a beginning, but we need help. We need someone outside ourselves, someone with wisdom greater than the thinking that got us here in the first place. We need wisdom to free us from reliance on patterns of survival that actually hinder our whole being, wisdom to guide us gently and patiently, wisdom to move us at a pace that is good for our whole self.

We are not looking to change but to be transformed. It is a whole new way of experiencing ourselves and our relationship to God and the world around us. This means learning to let go. For most of us, this is new territory.

Not Change but Transformation

Transformation makes more sense when we understand more clearly how our mind works to blind and bind us. We have reached this point in our lives by constructing a sense of ourselves out of abstract qualities ("I'm sincere," "I'm a happy person," or "I'm an intense person," and so on) and identifying ourselves with these constructs. We attach our worth and sense of self to them.

This approach leaves us attached to ideas and ideals, opinions and viewpoints, memories and reactive patterns that we identify as "me" or "my beliefs" or "my religion." Since these are built on intellectual concepts they divide everything in terms of either/or, good/bad, right/wrong, for me/against me, mine/yours, me/you. This mind-made sense of self leaves us defined in opposition to other "selves"; this is "me" and you are "not me." To hold onto this sense of a separate "me," our conceptual self needs to be in conflict with other selves. We begin to experience ourselves only in comparison or competition with one another.

To feel good about this self, to feel safe and secure, we need our ideas to be "the right ideas," which means that if you disagree you must be wrong. Since our security is built on these flimsy abstractions, we begin to look outside our self to make up for our inner lack of security. We feel we must protect what little we think we have. This car, this piece of land, or this personal quality is necessary to bolster our sense of self, which means that if anyone seems to threaten these in any way, something must be done about them. We are left feeling very fragile and easily threatened, a readily combustible mixture for violence.

As we grow older each of us becomes more accustomed to the personal perspective that helps us feel that we can understand, control, and relate to the world around us, as well as find some measure of comfort, security, and esteem. Because we need to feel in control of our lives as a substitute for our connection to God we believe that "this is the way it is." So we become distraught and defensive whenever somebody challenges our version of "this is the way it is."

Other people have another version of "this is the way it is." Their version is formed by their personality, background, personal experiences, and how they have learned to relate to these. They are just as sure, just as convinced, and just as sincere about their version as we are about our version.

Our attachment to our personal version of "the way things are" and to personal qualities, ideas, possessions, power, achievement, and esteem creates turbulence in our relationships. Unfortunately, this is merely the surface turbulence. Also present are a deeper churning of our accumulated personal traumas and the even deeper turmoil of the unhealed destructiveness and violence experienced by our whole human race.

Soul Suffering and the Pain Body

Teresa of Ávila talks about this accumulated trauma as "soul suffering"[3]; Thomas Keating talks about the "reservoir of traumas"[4]; and Eckhart Tolle talks about the "pain body."[5] These authors use these images for the deep inner pain that comes from and contributes to the violence all around us. We experience this violence in our relationships. We experience anger, judgments, fears, and anxieties flaring up within ourselves and our partners. We wonder where it comes from. Our reaction is more than the situation warrants; it is like we have stepped on an emotional land mine.

Eckhart Tolle's image of the pain body expresses this phenomenon more clearly for me. The pain body is an accumulation of the traumas and pains that we have suffered. These leave behind a residue that lives on, lodged in our body and reflected in our mind.

Some of us have suffered terribly and tragically. But even normal disappointments and misunderstandings contribute to our pain body. We just had a first Communion celebration here at Saint Michael's. The little girls were dressed like brides and the little boys wore suits. Our religious education director did a wonderful job of preparing them and training them for the ceremony.

At the end of Mass they processed down the aisle in front of Father John, our pastor. They were very solemn as they slowly walked down the aisle. Then, in the last ten feet they broke like a flock of birds in that kind of synchronized turn that flocks do in mid-air. The whole group ran as one to the table where their first Communion gifts were collected. The delight in their eyes as they walked off with their beautifully wrapped gifts was wonderful. Except for one girl; there was no beautifully wrapped gift for her. Instead her mother pulled two twenties out of her purse and handed them to her. I am sure forty dollars is more than many of the other gifts cost. But the look of disappointment, hurt, and anger in the girl's eyes told another story. My own reaction of sadness also says something about the disappointments that have accumulated in my own pain body. The pain body is made up of both the major and minor traumas of our lives.

This pain creates a negative energy field that occupies our body and mind. If we consider it as an invisible entity in its own right, we are closer to the truth. It feeds on any experience that resonates with its own kind of energy, anything that creates further pain in whatever form: anger, destructiveness, hatred, grief, emotional drama, violence, and even illness. With the pain body, we carry within ourselves a need for pain, drama, and conflict. This means that we become either a victim or a perpetrator of pain. We either want to inflict pain or to suffer pain.

Evidence of this accumulated pain is written all over the pages of our newspapers. Whether it's the yearly death count from murders within our cities or the wars and terrorism raging between countries, religions, and political ideologies, the pain body shows itself in many guises. Humanity continues to be soaked in blood and stained with tears. The pain body continues to reproduce itself in our flesh and blood.

The Cross Begins Our Healing

The ultimate rattling of the golden chain, the ultimate wake-up call and the most real possibility of becoming free and alive is the cross of Christ. For the cross of Christ begins healing the pain body in both its personal and collective incarnations.

The cross is the human wound brought to light. And on the cross is divine love incarnate, love that cannot be overcome by darkness, that cannot be driven away with hammers and nails. Love wounded so that it can heal all wounds.

The cross is also human fear and hatred incarnated, made excruciatingly real, concrete, and livid with anger. And on the cross divine love incarnated wraps human flesh and blood around suffering, refusing to pass the suffering on by retaliating.

> To any one who considers the immense love which Jesus Christ has shown us in his life, and especially in his death, it is impossible not to be stirred and excited to love a God who is so enamored of our souls.
>
> Saint Alphonsus Liguori[6]

Undoubtedly, the death of Jesus puts us between a rock and a hard place. It places us between the trauma of Jesus' death, the death of an innocent man hung out like a rag, and the mystery of our Father's love as it is trying to break through into our awareness. The cross is the consequence of the Father and Son's unconditional love for us and the consequence of all within us that fears love without condition and that distrusts love as a gift rather than an achievement.

The cross burns into our hearts the image of an innocent lover, who is so fully alive, so transfigured by our Father's love, that our fearful, defensive, half-dead hearts cannot endure it. All that is not fully alive within us shrinks in terror at the possibility that we could be loved this much, and even more alarming, that we could love this much. Jesus accepts the necessity of death in order to awaken us to kinship with himself, to awaken us to the Father as the center of our lives, rather than our fear-driven egos.

The cross draws on a deeper resource than mind and will to heal our blindness and free us from our bindings. Mind and will alone cannot provide enough motivation. It is not enough motivation for Jesus to understand the necessity of freeing us and desire to heal us. This would simply leave us with another dead hero.

In his love for his eternal Father and his compassionate love for us, his sisters and brothers, Jesus is impelled by the love that is the very source of creation, healing, and transformation. It is a love of compassion, union, oneness, a love that comes from a deeper source than even the best of intentions and the highest of ideals. This is love springing forth from the very essence of God.

> And just as Moses lifted up the serpent in the wilderness, so must the Son of Man be lifted up, that whoever believes in him may have eternal life. For God so loved the world that he gave his only Son, so that everyone who believes in him may not perish but may have eternal life.
>
> John 3:14–16

Because of his awareness of the eternity and intimacy of the Father's love, Jesus' suffering and death are a defiance of all that would reduce us to an object of anger, fear, and hate. Jesus does more than accept his fate; he participates in robbing its icy meaninglessness by clinging to our Father's eternal warmth. He truly is lifted up on the cross, a glorification of his Father.

No More Victims

This cross will not be used as a bully pulpit, as moral high ground, the victim ranting in righteous triumph, creating a whole new generation of victims. "Father, forgive them; for they do not know what they are doing" (Luke 23:34).

This is a mystical awareness. It is free of identification with anything but the Father's love. It is the freedom of one who knows himself to be the beloved child of the eternal and faithful Father. It is the heart of the Father bursting forth in the Son with love for all who suffer being blinded and bound.

This very action becomes the greatest manifestation of the Father, the Word become flesh and the silent Father pouring themselves as love into healing our awareness and our pain-bound hearts. The Father has always been with us as the intimate Creator of our being, but now the immensity and profundity of his love is unveiled in a way that turns any other word into meaningless chatter.

Blood is spilt on the cross in one more vain attempt to control God with sacrifice. But our Father will have none of this. In Jesus, blood is spilt to reach out to us. If we can respond in compassion for this innocent victim, maybe we can accept compassion for our naive, innocent, and misguided choices that have caused so much suffering in ourselves and others. Maybe we can accept the solidarity that binds us together into a new way of seeing ourselves as our Father's kingdom.

On the cross Jesus plunged into the reservoir of unresolved pain, suffering, and violence that soaks both our personal and collective unconscious. This plunge into the depths of hell begins healing the very roots of evil. His blood poured out as love for us courses through the heart of humanity as the only antidote that can transform the very inception of this most contagious and deadly of all diseases.

And in his resurrection Jesus brings all of creation into the healing light of unconditional love. As Saint Paul says: "...everything exposed by the light becomes visible, for everything that becomes visible is light. Therefore it says, 'Sleeper, awake!/Rise from the dead,/and Christ will shine on you'" (Ephesians 5:13–14).

This light brings a whole new clarity of vision. It unites our personal lives to Jesus' dying and rising. In dying we lose the blindness of our ego-mind and rise to the clarity of our true self. This is a higher dimension of consciousness, the blessedness Jesus calls us to in the Beatitudes; "Blessed are the pure in heart, for they will see God" (Matthew 5:8). This seeing frees us from our judgments to be present in unconditional love to all that is before us.

The clarity of seeing and the love on the cross exposes the demonic element of our shared pain body as it extends itself through inflicting and enduring ever more pain. The loving man on the cross whose innocence exposes this violence for what it is, strips away the façade of justice and righteousness that has hidden the bloodlines of violence from the beginning.

Our carefully constructed and compulsively sustained ego survival techniques are exposed by the light of the cross. From the cross Jesus calls our true self out of repression and hiding. The Son who knows himself as well as all of us to be "beloved," loved without limit or condition, and whose whole being is love for all creation, awakens us to kinship with himself and one another.

In the death of this divinely innocent human on the cross, the myth of a friendly and humanly meaningful world is also hung out to die. Paradoxically, this is where we find out what it truly means to be loved. We come to know the profound depth and breadth, and realism of the Father's love for us—a love that knows our divine origin as well as our limited and wounded humanness. This is not a naive love that overlooks our faults, nor the harsh consequences of our fear-based addictions. This is a love that loves us for all of who we are.

This love knows that we are desperately consumed with infinite desires that blind us to the immediacy and intimacy of our Father's unconditional, loving presence. This love knows that we fear healing and freedom because it means dying to all that binds us to a vain attempt to find comfort and security.

Loved for All of Who We Are

And we are loved on this cross, even though clinging to our ego-mind creates the violence that nailed Jesus to its wood. It is this clinging that gives rise to this bloody miscarriage of justice, to executions of blameless victims (both emotionally and physically), to betrayal in loyalty and fickleness in friendships, and to the cruel political expediencies that stain our personal, corporate, and national histories. The cross unites us both as perpetrators and victims. For we, too, suffer anguish, personal humiliations, and fears; we are betrayed, undergo loss and loneliness. All of this is united in the dying and rising of Jesus. He has chosen the suffering of the cross because we cannot avoid suffering.

When we try to be loving people, try to live by God's commandments and follow the lead of Jesus, as long as our ego is the only way we approach these values, we will bring the cross upon ourselves and others. The cross of Christ confronts us with our power and our helplessness, our power to inflict violence and pain, and our helplessness to do anything about it.

If we respond to the innocent man on the cross with great love, we will find that our most sincere efforts at being in control, being secure, and successful are useless in relieving his plight. In the light of his cross we find that we are even more helpless than he. And if we're lucky, if we're willing to accept the grace of this moment of powerlessness, we may find that Jesus' way through helplessness is our way through helplessness.

Powerlessness is full of grace. Helplessness is where God awaits us. Powerlessness and helplessness deflate our ego-mind of all its pretensions. When we are stripped of all the illusions of power, we find that we continue to exist and our continued existence is what we share with all of our sisters and brothers.

We all suffer; we all die. It doesn't matter if we're a Samaritan woman, a Roman centurion, a leper, a drunkard, a tax collector, or a woman caught in adultery. We all suffer and die. And God is present to every one of us, loving us eternally.

No one can claim this God as their sole possession, nor make this God a personal ally against their enemies. If they cause suffering, then God is there. The Word shares flesh with those who are made to suffer.

On the cross Jesus hung, arms outstretched, between a good thief and a bad thief, and they are bound together with him in death. Just as heaven and earth, human and divine, yin and yang, male body and female soul, power and powerlessness, forgiven and forgiving, loved and loving, even good and evil are all bound up in the divine flesh of this human son of the Prodigal Father, who runs toward all of us, arms stretched out in joy, calling "My child, who was dead, is alive."

The passion accounts in the gospels are charged with moments that shed light and possible healing on our human wounded powerlessness. There's that scene at the Last Supper where Peter declares, "I will lay down my life for you" (John 13:37). That's his ego talking. It's the way he wants to be, wants to identify himself and project himself (as the loyal and brave one). Little does he suspect the fear lurking behind the bravado. But Jesus knows him and loves him for who he is. And Jesus knows that his true chance is in being deflated. "I tell you, before the cock crows, you will have denied me three times" (John 13:38). Talk about rattling Peter's golden chain. This is his wake-up call. When the cock does crow, Peter sees the lie by which he has been bound and knows the truth about himself. This is a death that will find new life in his encounters with the risen Lord. This is the powerless moment that can lead to surrender to the intimately present Father.

Our world binds us to an impoverished version of our humanity and blinds us with a grotesque vision of what it means to be fully alive. But the whole thrust of Jesus' life and death is to awaken us, his sisters and brothers, to that place within ourselves that is open to the life-giving Father.

We Continue to Be the Resurrection

The resurrection of Jesus is more than a happy ending to an unspeakable tragedy. Instead, the resurrected Christ continues in our lives. We become the flesh of the Word who makes the Father manifest. This is not an easy transition for us. There is no resurrection without dying. We, too, must give up our ego-driven lives to live resurrected life. Jesus leads us through death as the way to new life.

I used to summarize the meaning of the cross for myself in this way: "There is no death without resurrection." But now this is turned around for me: "There is no resurrection without death." We will "live through" the experience of death to our ego-mind so that we might be transformed to a freedom and love that will make everything before seem like a ghost. The resurrection is the meaning of the cross, just as the cross is the meaning of the resurrection. There is no death without resurrection and there is no resurrection without death.

We do ourselves a disservice when we think we can explain the cross or resurrection, turn them into an event or dogma, and spare ourselves from experiencing them as the fabric of our own lives. Jesus cannot be reduced to a mere example of how to live the divine life in human form. He is that life continuing the mystery of the Father's love in our dying and rising. His story and our story are one. We

> *The water that I will give will become in them a spring of water gushing up to eternal life.*
>
> John 4:14

are inside his story and its meaning is being created within our lives. The passion accounts do not give us meaning; they bring us to meaning, from inside, like the spring of life-giving waters.

As this spring wells up within us it brings life to all that it waters. The mud of human living becomes the clay vessel of the divine spirit. Death becomes life, helplessness is the place of God's power, and darkness is transformed into light.

We return to the Letter to the Ephesians because it reveals the profound transformation that is Christ.

> *For once you were darkness, but now in the Lord you are light. Live as children of light—for the fruit of the light is found in all that is good and right and true. Try to find out what is pleasing to the Lord. Take no part in the unfruitful works of darkness, but instead expose them. For it is shameful even to mention what such people do secretly; but everything exposed by the light becomes visible, for everything that becomes visible is light. Therefore it says, "Sleeper, awake!/Rise from the dead,/and Christ will shine on you."*
>
> EPHESIANS 5:8–14

Anything brought into the light becomes light. Modern psychology tells us that healing happens when our shadow is brought into the light of consciousness. Spirituality tells us that nonjudgmental awareness and love are the light that frees our true self. And the cross reveals that evil is transformed. Goodness is not just evil avoided or denied, this would be just another creation of our dualistic mind. "For God all things are possible" (Matthew 19:26). Evil, suffering, powerlessness, fear, and shame can all be transformed in the light of Christ. In the domain of the divine sin and salvation are not opposites, they are correlatives. The shame of the cross is the triumph of love.

> *...whenever I am weak, then I am strong.*
> 2 Corinthians 12:10

The shame of the cross is the triumph of love. Shame, cross, powerlessness, triumph, and love are uneasy companions in our mind, but they find a peaceful dwelling in the living, dying, and rising that is Jesus, the Jesus who continues in our lives.

The Cross Means More Than Anything We Can Say About It

We have been looking at the cross through a kaleidoscope. Every turn creates a new pattern of meaning. There is no insight, idea, feeling, or dogma that can express the meaning of this tragic death of an innocent man. Nothing we use to interpret it is big enough to carry its meaning—not grief, nor pity, nor compassion, not even outrage can contain the cross. We feel an echo of this in the death of our loved ones. No matter what we say to console ourselves, it is not enough; it is just something to say to keep our mind off the grief.

Paradoxically, when we are willing to accept the futility of any explanation, we can be drawn into the meaning of Jesus' living, dying, and rising. In letting go of our minds, our feelings, our ego, our self as the source of meaning, we can surrender to the Father as our source. With Jesus we find that we receive new life only by surrendering. We become not "self-less" but surrendered. We are enabled to exist on a plane where our Father and our true self are free to come and go, to share an intimate friendship without restraint or fear. This is what Jesus' disciples found to be their truth.

The disciples' hopes for Jesus died on the cross. They had hoped for a powerful Messiah who could turn stones into bread and be protected by God's angels. They thought that they had attached themselves to a Messiah whose shirttails they could ride into a new kingdom of riches, fame, glory, and power.

When their hopes died their small self, their ego-mind, also died and for the first time they were able to see and hear from their hearts. Their golden chain was broken along with their hopes. For the first time they came to know the hidden treasure of the Father's intimate and creative love bursting forth within them. They began to catch on that they, too, might be "my beloved child" and they rose with Jesus. For they, too, must wrap their flesh and blood around divinity so that they can carry on the work he began. Crosses stand all around us, shrouding our world, throbbing with the human wound, and aching for a healing heart.

Like the disciples, we will continue the healing of the pain body in our own lives. We will be led, in our Father's wise and patient love, to let go of our ego-mind and live from our true self. Ours is an incredible vocation. We are not merely witnesses to the passionate love of the Father and Son, we are the continuation of that love. We are created from the heart of the Father, the continued manifestation of the Son, and guided into wholeness and freedom by the Spirit, to be partners in incarnating the kingdom of God. Anything else falls short of our divine-human heritage.

Who We Are Because of Who God Is: The Spirituality of the Cross

Who are we?

The cross is the Father and Son's determination to meet us where we are, love us for who we are, and open us to healing and wholeness. Jesus chose to suffer because we cannot avoid suffering. By plunging into suffering and death Jesus exposes the ultimate illusion of separation from our Father. This is the pivotal revelation that every person is one who is of God, from God, and held close to God's heart through all adversity—forever. Nothing can separate us from the love of God.

At the same time, the cross reveals the stark reality of our condition: we are both perpetrators and victims. We, too, suffer anguish, personal humiliations, and fears; we are betrayed, undergo loss and loneliness. We are vulnerable to violence and this leaves us vulnerable to doing violence, even to the most innocent of all victims. We have the power to inflict violence yet we have little power to do anything about it.

We are the ones who are in need of healing salvation.

In the tragedy, the murder of this innocent, loving, and compassionate man, we are freed from a simplistic understanding of ourselves—freed to a true compassion that allows us to bond with the helpless and fully alive Savior on the cross.

We are the ones who learn that Jesus' way through helplessness is our way through helplessness. On the cross we meet the helpless one who is everything that we want to avoid—brokenness, poverty, failure, shame—as we cling to our self for safety and to our self-appropriated qualities for value. Here our culture of achievement, honor, and affluence is laid aside and defenses are abandoned for a seemingly reckless abandonment to the living God. The whole thrust of Jesus' life is distilled in his death in which he opens himself to letting go, to being fully alive in his Father.

We are the ones who find that everything we cling to for strength is weakness and the only way out is to let go of our perceived strength and surrender to the Father whom we encounter in our weakness.

On the cross love remains unconditionally present even in the face of the destructive fear, the wound that we bear. For this is exactly where we need to be healed by unconditional love.

We are the ones who are loved for all of who we are. This is not a naive love that overlooks our faults, nor the harsh consequences of our fear-based addictions.

We are the ones whose minds cannot encompass the love on the cross, let alone the faithful Father who will not abandon us.

When we are willing to accept the futility of any explanation, we can be drawn into the meaning of Jesus' death and resurrection. We find that we receive new life only by surrendering our old life-ego-mind.

We are the ones for whom powerlessness, suffering, death, and even evil are ripe with eternal presence, able to burst forth into fresh life—a life so different from the old that only our true self can recognize its continuity. Our mind melts before this reality and leaves us utterly vulnerable to the silence of pure Love, one in being with the Father.

Who we are only makes sense because of whose we are.

chapter 4

The Eucharist

To Be on Earth Partners to the Father, the Body of Christ, and Tutored by the Spirit

When I was six I fell in love with the night sky. I loved to lay on my back, the old wool blanket steeped in its mothball smell keeping me from the dampness of the grass. I lay there and stared as hard as I could into the stars. I was looking for God.

I could usually talk Johnny Bill into stargazing with me. You need to talk about these things. They are not as wonderful when they are only in your head. And having somebody else with you also means that you can make up stories together, travel the galaxies, and explore the moon to find out if it really is made of cheese. Wouldn't our parents be proud when we became spacemen! Later, when President Kennedy was shot, the moon took on his image, just like that of Lincoln on a penny.

"Do you think they could be twenty, maybe thirty, maybe even a hundred miles up there?" That's about as far as I could imagine. I'd seen planes flying over, and they must have been two or three hundred feet up there. A long way when you're six years old.

But then Uncle Floyd told us about "light-years." He'd read it in *National Geographic*. You could never quite tell if Uncle Floyd was making it up, or if it was true. I thought he was kidding on this one. Light-years! That's way too far.

Now that I'm older, and educated, and believe in light-years, the stars are just as awesome. As a kid I wondered who God could be, to be even bigger than the whole universe.

And when my mother told me that God, who is bigger than even the universe, knows about me, loves me, cares about me, and protects me, I faced something that made even less sense than light-years. Except that it was my mother telling me, and she didn't kid. A little of the marvel was tarnished when I went to school and found out that God loves me only when I pay attention, and do my homework, and don't fight.

Now, on the side of a mountain in Tucson, Arizona, the stars are just as bright as they were to my child eyes. Once again I can see all the little pinprick stars, even farther out there than the light-year stars.

But here in the desert the wonder of this clear, star-clamored night has to be shared with the savage, primal praise, joy, and thanksgiving of coyotes exulting in their kill. Once again the pack shares food. It sends a whole different kind of shiver down my spine. In a moment of terror, some animal has just died, to be a meal that the coyotes celebrate with a howling, triumphal chorus.

It was in the desert that God shaped the Hebrews into his people. And it was in the desert that Jesus, led by the Spirit, let go of his ordinary means of survival to choose his Father as the center of his life. In his living, preaching, healing, dying, and rising, Jesus takes us, along with his disciples, into a spiritual desert, where our old ways of survival no longer work, and we must learn to see with a vision cleared of prejudice and judgments.

The desert, with its mixture of silence and awe and hostility, is the training ground for spiritual awakening. In the desert we must pay attention to reality as it is and let go of our obscured perceptions if we want to survive. A plant that looks soft and fuzzy is actually a cactus with razor-sharp thorns. Nothing in the desert says "hug me." Javelinas look like wild pigs but are really rodents. They shy away from humans but will attack if they sense their young are in danger. And they can chew through a prickly pear cactus, spiked thorns and all. Nothing is as simple as it looks.

In the Eucharist Jesus takes us into the desert where nothing is as simple as it looks. At Mass the howling coyote is replaced by an infant indignant with hunger or the joyful shout of a baby thrilling to the acoustics. If you could listen to the stories of the people around you, you would hear of suffering and heroism camouflaged in the ordinary and seemingly familiar. Listen to the lector and you don't know if they have overcome fear to serve the community in their reading, or are trying to overcome the need to be the center of attention so that they might serve the word they proclaim. A quiet and serene person may just have nothing going on or may have made peace with his or her demons. You cannot tell by what you see. But know this, every bit of this is crammed with Divine Presence.

This and That Side of the Altar

When I'm on vacation, I go to Mass on "this side of the altar." It is a totally different experience than when I am the presider, on the other side of the altar. This side is a lot noisier. There is so much going on: getting babies settled, looking for friends, or for gossip. On the other side, it is calmer, quieter. As presider I have a chair with plenty of room on all sides.

On this side we are at the whim of the presider. We participate in his mood, which creates the backdrop against which everything else is seen and felt and meant. Or we get enmeshed in the distractions all around us, relegating the presider to background noise like the TV's blathering in our homes.

On the other side, as presider, I choose how much and to what I will respond. I begin by looking for people who look like they want to be here, like we're in this together. On this side there is not much choice. I am surrounded by moods and motivations that have nothing to do with me.

The last time I was in Omaha and went to Mass with my parents, I realized how different the two sides of the altar are. I have been so caught up in my own expectations of what "should" be and my experiences from the other side of the altar that I didn't realize how distant and insulated some people are from what is going on behind the lectern and altar. We sat among families who spent the whole time arbitrating the squabbles between their children and comforting their crying infants. And the children spent the whole time annoying one another.

Clearly, what was going on up front was not all that important. From the outside it seemed to me that when the adults get bored they turned their attention to their children—which tells me what is most important to them. And yet these families were here. God only knows how much effort went into feeding, dressing, and gathering their family for this Mass. Maybe in their lives Divine Presence and their children intermingle.

In the midst of all this I retreated into my childhood memories of going to Mass with my family where I dreaded the boredom and learned the first litany prayer of my life: "Is it over yet?" Only as an adult, well removed in years, can I wrap enough nostalgia around those moments to invest them as sacred memories. Mostly I was putting in time.

I don't know when this boredom and noninvolvement changed for me. It certainly was not when I was first ordained. At that time I felt like I had to entertain the congregation or pep them up, anything to get them into the Mass, which meant I was not in it. I was trying to make up for what I felt was lacking in my own experience of attending. But somehow the Mass began to become a prayer and ever more importantly, our prayer—not just my private prayer or my responsibility, but praying happening between us and to us.

On that Sunday in Omaha, as I sat with my parents, on this side of the altar, drowning in noise and distraction, I wondered how this prayer that was bigger than all of us could become possible for both sides of the altar. It had to have already happened, because on that side it couldn't happen without this side. Somehow the ordinary chaos of family life and the mystery of Trinitarian presence inhabit the same space.

> *When he was at the table with them, he took bread, blessed and broke it, and gave it to them. Then their eyes were opened, and they recognized him; and he vanished from their sight. They said to each other, "Were not our hearts burning within us while he was talking to us on the road, while he was opening the scriptures to us?"*
>
> LUKE 24:30–32

If the stars can bring us closer to God and make "our hearts burn within us," then we must all be natural liturgists with a built-in sense of wonder that can respond to the immediacy of divine presence in the "breaking of the bread" as well as ordinary life. If we can attend Mass weekly, penetrate the commotion around us, find food for our faith, and let the Scriptures open to us, we must be filled with the Divine.

The trap of trying to foster better worship might be too much reliance on mind and will with its need to judge according to abstract expectations. Burning hearts are not created through intellectual combustion; they are ignited in response to one another and to the mystery in which we all exist. The Trinitarian outpouring of love is such a normal element of our very ordinary lives that we miss its reality until the Mass exposes it in the bread and wine—ordinary food and drink that is at the same time "my body" and "the cup of my blood,...It will be shed for you and for all...."[1]

When we experience the sacred depth of our ordinary lives, we come to know that all the ordinary is an expression of the extraordinary. This is the awareness to which the desert brings us by making us hyperaware of our surroundings while necessitating the letting go of our old ways of thinking.

Tony Hendra, in his tribute to Father Joe Warrilow, an English Benedictine monk, describes the moment at Communion when he awakened to the extraordinary reality of his ordinary life:

> As I took the host..., all the conflicting and confus-ing thoughts and feelings I normally experienced,... were swept aside, fused into a whole of certainty. It...all made perfect sense—this was bread just as Christ had used bread, this was a meal just as the Last Supper had been; how else would you take your God into yourself but through your mouth, consum-ing him in this ordinary, mundane way? The ordi-nary was the divine.[2]

Living as Trinity

At Mass we celebrate the wonder of our lives as we become aware of them immersed in the mystery of the Creator's transforming love. A love made known in Jesus Christ and patiently coming to fruition through the inspiration of Holy Spirit. We recall Jesus' life and death in the past so that we can understand the presence of God working in and through our lives here and now. We celebrate our lives as the ordinary expression of the extraordinary Trinity.

To praise, to give thanks, to glorify are all ways of let-ting go and letting the extraordinary fill our living. The focus is the Father whose faithfulness is the reason we can let go. As the Spirit moves in us, gently relaxing our grip, we can become partners in the kingdom that is coming alive because of the Father's generosity, the Son's compassion, the Spirit's wisdom, and our openness.

The kingdom that comes alive as we relate more intimately with the Father is the focus of Jesus' preaching. Since this kingdom is primarily a relationship, it is proclaimed most fully in the way Jesus reached out to people. One of his basic ways of reaching out was in sharing meals and stories.

> *If God were a theory, the study of theology would be the way to understand God. But God is alive and in need of love and worship.*
> Abraham Joshua Heschel[3]

The gospels abound with memories of Jesus sitting around a table, sharing stories and a meal with friends, Pharisees, women, tax collectors, prostitutes, Samaritans, and all kinds of people. These meals and their stories include all these people because the kingdom includes all these people. Sharing bread, drinking from a common cup were the way that Jesus both expressed and created the relationship these meals incarnated.

This eating and drinking culminated in Jesus' Last Supper. At this supper Jesus did what he had done so many times before—he "took the bread" and "raised his eyes to heaven," he gave thanks and "said the blessing," the *berekah*.

At this supper, however, he envisions and intends a whole new reality. He takes the bread and names it "my body." He thanks his Father for this gift, which he is going to give for the life of the world. Evidently the Spirit, who drove Jesus out into the desert, is back at work, inspiring the coming of the kingdom in ways that no one could have imagined. The human-divine, ordinary-extraordinary genuineness of this moment is made eternally present here and now.

Digesting Mystery

On the night in which he stands most in need of inner reassurance and courage, Jesus taps into the story that would connect him more consciously to the gracious love he knew to be his Father. It was the ancient story and ritual of the Passover meal that anointed these moments with meaning sufficient to meet the unpredictability of what was to come.

The Hebrew people had learned in their struggle and suffering the sureness of God's faithfulness. In the story of their Passover, succeeding generations would be guided through their own deserts to find the divine

> *Over every living thing which is to spring up, to grow, to power, to ripen during this day, say again the words: This is my Body. And over every death-force which waits in readiness to corrode, to wither, to cut down, speak again your commanding words...This is my blood.*
>
> Pierre Teilhard de Chardin[4]

presence of compassion, forgiveness, love, and joy that lie in the depths of their hearts. Jesus called this breaking through of the divine into our awareness the *kingdom of God*. This time, in this kingdom we are to be fed, not the manna that faded away, but the bread and wine, body and blood, the source of divine life nourishing our lives eternally.

Jesus' story is about our future as it is being created in our present. At the table of the kingdom, it becomes the meaning of our story and we are blessed when our own lives become the resurrected body of Christ. We are transformed as the meaning of our lives is revealed in the events of Jesus' living, dying, and rising.

The very nature of the way Jesus saves us demands ritual. Jesus' preaching and life bring us into an intimate relationship with our Father and through our Father with one another. His total giving of himself draws us into a transformation that must be ritualized so that our woundedness can be gently and patiently healed and our true selves freed to respond as partners in his kingdom.

This healing and transformation involve much more than simply hearing or even accepting a new truth. It entails relating to our Father with the same intimacy and generous trust as Jesus. Jesus wants us to share in the Father's divine consciousness and unconditional loving. He wants our whole being to be ignited by the Spirit, as he is. And he wants us to be incorporated as a community incarnating his own compassion and compunction for all our brothers and sisters, especially those who, like us, are least able to help themselves.

> ...[L]iturgy continually confronts us with the call to sacrifice our preoccupation with self. Because liturgy is intrinsically corporate, it resists any narrowing of the spiritual life to a private relationship between the solitary soul and God. Liturgy places God in the center and us in community.
>
> John S. Mogabgab[5]

So Jesus invites us to share this banquet ritual, knowing that we will need to immerse ourselves in it over and over. We accept his invitation when we respond with faith and love—both actions of giving and letting go of our self as we focus on the Father as our possibility. In choosing to pray with a community, we let go of our protective boundaries. In choosing to focus on our Father's agenda, we lay our ego aside. In both instances, we are opening ourselves to becoming a whole new reality—the kingdom.

Ritual works by enkindling within our imaginations hope in a life and a story that is greater than the story we have chosen for ourselves. At the same time it works in our hearts by allowing the Spirit to melt our constricting fears and anger, and free our true self to fill the void left by our ego.

This God will never abandon us or allow us to abandon our selves or divine intimacy. Like the Son we are embraced by the Father. We eat the Son's body and drink his blood so that we can become what we eat and drink. Eating and drinking with him, we hear the meaning of our life told in his life story. We become children of God, children of love by feeding on love.

We are not able to digest this immense mystery the first time, or the second. That is why Jesus left us with a ritual, a celebration in which we celebrate this intimacy in the bread and the cup and retell the story of who we are being created to be in the many situations we find ourselves. Our lives continue to grow and transform because God's generosity is always faithful.

Ritual Elements From Jesus' Own Jewish Spirituality

In most of our lives there are elements of the eucharistic ritual that grab our imagination and open us to personal meaning. The priest prays during the Offertory ritual as he adds a drop of water to the wine that we, through the water and wine, may ourselves share in the divinity of Christ, just as he shared in our humanity. That image, and those words, have remained fresh for me. The image and the words mingle to express a bonding with Jesus that takes me beyond words into meaning and mystery. It is like a song in which the melody carries the words beyond their meaning.

One ritual element central to Jesus' relationship with our Father was the *berekah*. The *berekah* is a traditional Jewish form of blessing, thanksgiving, and praise. Its very form connects us to an awareness of God in the concreteness of our lives. It recalls what God has done for us, and then trusting in his faithfulness, it asks God to continue what he has done in the new circumstances of our life.

This prayer captures the foundations of the Hebrew faith in God, their appreciation, and gratitude because he has done so much for them. It offers praise, thanks, and glory to God who brought them out of the slavery of Egypt. Praise, thanks, and glory to God who made them his own people in the desert and brought them into the Promised Land. Praise, thanks, and glory to God who blessed them with the Law that gave order to their life. Praise, thanks, and glory to the God who continued to be with them in the struggles and suffering of life. In the challenges of life they found God faithfully creating the compassion, forgiveness, love, and joy that got them through all their deserts.

In his faithfulness God continues what he began with their ancestors. Their gratitude and appreciation for this faithful God keeps them aware of and appreciative of God as the source of all that is good in their life. This same attitude continues in our lives through humble gratitude. It is that deeply felt awareness that we can trust God because God has been so much for us. We can see this in Jesus' relationship to his Father.

On the occasion when the crowds were waiting to be fed and the resources for feeding were minimal, Jesus turned his sights on the Father, and in gratitude he took the bread, raised his eyes to heaven, gave thanks, and said the *berekah*. When the earthly gifts, made of human hands, seemed inadequate, he turned to the abundant Source of all creation.

And at the Last Supper when his loyal followers' confidence was inadequate, he again gave all that is happening into the Father's hands and prayed, *berekah*. How human and how divine his response. As he names the bread "my body" and gives it into our hands, we are brought to participate in it as our reality. Taking the wine, knowing that his blood will soon be shed, he gives us the cup of "my blood." When we take and receive, our lives, like Jesus', are given into the Father's hands.

Against this background one of Jesus' earlier statements is tinged with new meaning:

*"Therefore I tell you, do not worry about your life,
what you will eat or what you will drink, or about
your body, what you will wear. Is not life more than
food, and the body more than clothing? Look at the
birds of the air; they neither sow nor reap nor gather
into barns, and yet your heavenly Father feeds them.
Are you not of more value than they?"*

MATTHEW 6:25–26

"Life" and "body" in this passage mean the same thing
as "body and blood." They refer to the whole of who we
are, our reality, which comes to us directly from God and
is the living, pulsating experience of God's love for us. The
redeeming power of God's love is always here for all of us.
But we have to be willing to believe it, accept it to the point
that we give up trying to sustain ourselves, trying to make
ourselves exist. When we can give that up, let go and let God,
everything changes. Our life becomes a blessing, praise, and
thanksgiving.

The ritual of the Eucharist calls us to trust our Father's
faithfulness and surrender into his hands. When we do this,
we meet the Father's determination to rescue us from our
deadly, frightened refusal to love and be loved. We meet it
in the flesh and blood of Jesus' willingness to give himself as
our body and blood. "This bread is my body, this cup is my
blood," gives a new depth of meaning to "...do not worry
about your life, what you will eat or what you will drink, or
about your body" (Matthew 6:25). The inner heart of God
is unveiled as the bread and wine become the flesh and blood
of the Christ, the firstborn from the dead. We live because
Christ lives. We live forever because we are loved forever. We
live forever, in the eternity that begins now, because we are
fed at our Father's table. We let go of our self-circumscribed
world to become partners in the universal world of our Creator.

The Eucharist Makes Us Really Present

The Eucharist does not so much "render" Christ in his living, dying, and rising present to us as it helps us be present to him.

Again, the blessing prayer, *berekah,* has something to teach us. In this prayer we thank God for all that he has given us and we bring it before him trusting that he is faithful. And in his faithfulness he will continue to be generous. In other words, he will continue to shower us with his abundance. We are thankful, and in our trust we open ourselves to the divine, the spiritual, the eternal intimacy of the Trinity. We get back more than we had in the first place. We bring ourselves, receive bread and wine, and are transformed into Jesus' living body. When we become involved with God we are led into the fullness of our being. When we eat ordinary food it becomes us. When we eat divine food we become divine. We walk away from the table with more than we came.

This all hinges on an act of faith. We start with material gifts, gifts we can see and taste, smell and feel, and we walk away with a spiritual gift. Faith is the trust that opens our whole being to God's possibilities in our own life.

"Opening our whole being" in faith is easy to say but elusive in its simplicity. In my life I can see that "faith" has gone through a metamorphosis. When I was young, sitting next to my parents in church, *faith* meant trusting them and learning what they believed. A pivotal time for internalizing faith came in college.

I studied philosophy and after three years I came to a point where I felt that I could prove, at least to my satisfaction, that God exists and also that God does not exist. I could make a plausible argument for either side.

This left me with a dilemma. I had to choose on which side I wanted to stake my happiness, and philosophy wasn't going to help me. It left the responsibility with me.

That seemed unfair. At that time three years of thinking seemed like a lifetime. Frankly, I was depressed by the whole thing. I had never put that much work into anything, and I wasn't about to put any more effort into it.

Except that I was haunted by a simple question: "Why?" Why can't faith be proven? Why does it demand a risk, or as Søren Kierkegaard put it, "a leap of faith."[6] I had no answer at all and no energy to continue thinking. I gave up.

And in giving up, something floated up from within, into my awareness; like the message in one of those magic eight balls we played with as kids. Here is what floated up, "the risk is necessary because faith must start with hope and love," with giving rather than grasping. The risk involved in letting go of certainty and letting go of my expectation demands for God, was, without knowing it, dying and rising.

The risk meant letting go to see if I could rely on God. It meant giving to God the little I had so that it could be transformed into faith. It meant letting go of my reality so that I could be swept up into God's reality. And it meant letting go so that I could be present to what is truly real.

How do we become present to Jesus at the table of the Eucharist? We come as a sacrifice, as giving up and letting go of what little we have. What we have to "let go" is so little: wealth, power, success, honor, virtue, a list of qualities that describe us in comparison to others. Even our best of intentions have little substance. All of these offer the illusion of happiness, but they do not satisfy our real needs.

In letting go we see through to a new way of organizing and valuing the world of experiences. Those things that attract so much of our energy begin to seem flimsy. We let go of all the things we cling to and find the gift of our indescribable self and source in God. We learn from Jesus as he gives himself to be our transformation into his resurrected body. We continue as the resurrected body of Christ. We are plunged into our own reality, which we find to be an expression of the Trinity.

A Community of Presence

We experience this new reality taking over our lives as we "give up" and "let go" of our judgments to be with a community of people who, like us, bring every bit of their humanness to the situation. It is not an abstract or antiseptic community that is brought together for worship. In accepting the noise, the coughing, and the shuffling, in making room for all the ways faith manifests itself in individuals, we make room within ourselves to receive and give from the largesse of the Trinity.

In this community we worship among the cares and concerns of parents; the awkward uncertainties of the young; the loneliness, grief, and impairment of the elderly. We are connected to the human web of suffering and need for healing and forgiveness. The cross is still very real in this world.

> *In each of our lives Jesus comes as the bread of life—to be eaten, to be consumed by us. This is how he loves us. Then Jesus comes in our human life as the hungry one, the other, hoping to be fed with the bread of our life, our hearts loving and our hands serving.*
> Mother Teresa of Calcutta[7]

We bring our own faith, hopes, and inklings of love. In the commitment of being together, and through this bonding in faith, we place our willingness and our resources on the table. We also place our broken words, our burdens, pain, suffering, death—both the little deaths and physical deaths. We offer the stuff of ordinary lives and get life back again—through food. We are not made holy by abstractions but by what is as much food and drink as we are flesh and blood. And that transforms our lives into Christ's resurrected body. We meet divinity in the humanity of our world.

Much of what touches our lives during the celebration

of the Eucharist relates to the most concrete realities: bread and wine, body and blood, the variety of people who are gathered together, each with their own needs, desires, and perspectives. I heard that one of the reasons G. K. Chesterton became a Catholic was that he saw a sign in the back of a Catholic church that read "Ladies, hold onto your purses. There are thieves among us." His comment was "If there is room for thieves here, there has to be room for a scoundrel like me."[8] Like all stories, it doesn't matter much if it is factual, because it is true.

Saint Michael of Old Town, in Chicago, is the parish where I live and minister. Many of the parishioners are between twenty-five and forty years old. The most populated Mass is at 7:00 PM on Sunday. Its known throughout Chicago as "the bar without booze." A popular activity after Mass is a take-off on the tradition of pilgrimage, called a "Tavern Tour." I love to preach at this Mass because the community listens so intensely. But many are also here to meet a potential mate. What could be more human and more sacred and more expressive of the mystery we celebrate?

This is indicative of the transforming grace of the Eucharist. It creates a new consciousness, a new way of seeing what is truly important about one another,

> *Eucharist is who we are. If you are the body of Christ and members of it, then it is that mystery which is placed on the Lord's table: you receive the mystery, which is to say the body of Christ, your very self. You answer Amen to who you are and in the answer you embrace yourself. You hear body of Christ and answer Amen. Be a member of Christ's body, that your amen will be true.*
>
> Saint Augustine[9]

ourselves, and the ordinariness of our lives. Our way of organizing and valuing our world is turned inside out. We are able to see beyond the concrete and obvious of the visible world into the sacredness of our ordinary lives.

Our visible spectrum now includes that vital energy that

gives life to the grape and the grain. It is this same vitality that transforms the bread and wine into the body and blood of Christ and the body and blood of Christ into our lives. And it is the same vitality that draws men and women to seek relationships outside their families, and husbands and wives to rejoice in their children, and children to grow up and let go of their family to be part of a new family, and all of us to "give up" and "let go" so that we make take our place in our divine family. We have begun to embrace the paradoxical message that life begins at the moment we die to our self.

This is what it means to be partners in the Trinity's great work of creating the kingdom. This is what it means to live in the presence of the Trinity, the One God who is transcendently awesome, immanently approachable, and wondrously incarnate. As the Father pours out his love in creation, and the Son manifests that love in his living, dying, and rising, we are filled with the Spirit and inspired to live the Son's human/divine story as our own. Looking at this ritual combination of ordinary people and simple elements from the outside, who would ever believe the extraordinary graciousness working within us?

Sacrifice and Surrender:
Divine Love Becomes Human Identity

Classical spirituality talks about this "giving up" and "letting go" as surrender to the will of God. In the Eucharist we talk about this surrender as sacrifice.

Unfortunately, we have been given a literal understanding of sacrifice and have lost the richness of its true meaning. Sacrifice conjures up images of bleating sheep, blood flowing from their throats, and smoking pyres of charred meat: all in an attempt by the worshiper to appease and manipulate the gods. It is a way of bargaining and bribing a fearsome and threatening god.

This is not the God of Jesus. Not the Father who takes the initiative to reach out to us. Not the relationship that draws us into itself so that we can join Jesus in living, dying, and rising as partners in the kingdom.

Instead of God accepting us because of our "sacrifice," we meet the Father and Son sacrificing themselves for us. In the living, dying, and rising of Jesus, the Father is the one who draws near to us. It is through the Father's generosity that we have bread and wine, and when we surrender it to the Father, it is through the Father's generosity, the Son's compassion, and the Spirit's blessing, that the bread and wine become Christ living, dying, and rising within us.

We surrender by accepting God as the center of our lives, as the one who nourishes our dreams and desires. We surrender the comfort of our image of God to accept this intense, immense love. And we surrender by allowing ourselves to become caught up in the eternal relationship of the Trinity.

We surrender by letting go of our private little worlds so that we can belong to this community where Christ ceaselessly gives himself for the transformation of the world. We surrender our kingdom to become a partner in creating the Trinity's kingdom. The sacrifice is that of the Father and Son. We surrender in grateful acceptance. We surrender to open our hearts to the Father and Son's sacrifice and continue to give it our flesh and blood.

The effect of accepting this love is a whole new image of our self, other persons, and the way the world is structured. To be loved so profoundly and so securely, beyond all the circumstances of our conditions and qualities, satisfies the deepest longings of our human hearts. This releases the energy we have committed to the tasks of defending and augmenting our sense of self. Our identity now comes from being loved rather than attempting to make our self lovable. We know ourselves as a gift rather than a project.

To be loved so much allows us to experience ourselves in

a whole new way. When we let go of our identification with the abstract qualities and roles of our circumstantial life, we begin to experience our interior core. We know ourselves as a subject and source of freely flowing energy. We know ourselves as inherently good, worthy of respect, and having a purpose in creation. Most importantly, we know that this is not our "doing" but our "being" created from the heart of love.

Since we know others as we know ourselves, we are now free to see others, and God, as subjects—no longer relegated to objects by our defensive needs. In our shared humanness this means that we experience our human woundedness with compassion rather than pity or disgust. As recipients of divine living, we know God with profound and humble gratitude rather than manipulative groveling or condescending conformity.

We are able to know this because now there is energy available to know unencumbered by prejudices and expectations. We no longer need to protect and project ourselves or strive to assert ourselves. We experience ourselves as a surplus of freely flowing energy, springs of living waters, branches of the living vine.

Learning to "Do This in Memory of Me"

The Eucharist does not merely set an abstract ideal before us, but it plunges us into its concrete reality. The purpose of the Eucharist is not just to bring about the real presence of Christ in bread and wine. The ultimate purpose is to let Christ turn us into his living body and blood so that all those who hunger to be loved and loving are fed with love.

We come to this table to meet Jesus who told us to remember "this is my body and this is my blood." But this is not the Jesus of 2000 years past. This is Jesus as he is now—in our sisters and brothers gathered around this table. This is the Jesus who we meet in our neighbors next door and on the other side of the world. This is the Jesus who is the extraordinary depth of our ordinary lives. We come together because we are flesh and blood and we need flesh and blood to mediate our spiritual reality. We are spiritual beings in human form, and we need human form to express and experience our spiritual reality.

> *In Holy Communion we have Christ under the appearance of bread. In our work we find him under the appearance of flesh and blood. It is the same Christ.*
> Mother Teresa of Calcutta[10]

Eucharist is where we learn to "do this in memory of me"—where we learn to become his body and blood, where we learn to let our lives be broken and our blood poured out for one another as partners in the kingdom, and where we learn that new life comes from letting go.

Transformed With the Bread and Wine Into the Body and Blood of Christ

In the Eucharist we are also being tutored into unity by being in relationship. What could be more unified than a community of people who have surrendered their small lives to rise with Christ into a new consciousness of being loved eternally and divinely? Here we come to know the common good as uncommonly good. Together we are being led into the very mystery of the Trinity.

Just as the Trinity is many though one, we find our many selves existing as one. The scandal of the cross, the love that is too hard to believe, is our shared fate. Who would dare claim that such an ordinary, limited, and wounded assembly of people are the continuing revelation of God's unconditional love, mercy, and forgiveness for the world?

Here again, the pagan notion of sacrifice has done us a disservice. When we attend the Eucharist as an offering to

God in order to obtain favors, we attend as individuals. We are taking care of our own needs. Saving our souls. Since the priest is doing the "sacrifice" for us, our attendance easily becomes mechanical. We relegate ourselves to performing our part in the ritual, standing up, kneeling, sitting down, saying the words we have memorized. In this way, we distance our self from God, who is now a means to salvation rather than a partner in transformation.

The pagan notion of sacrifice has also reduced our awareness of Christ's presence by focusing exclusively on his "real presence" in the bread and wine. Recently we have been trying to recover the breath and concreteness of God's love through recognizing Christ's presence also in the Scriptures, the worshiping community, and the presider in all of his humanness. This dramatically broadens our understanding of the lavishness of the Eucharist.

Now we attend the Eucharist to receive the body and blood of Christ in the fullness of its meaning. We take part in a meal in which we are filled with Christ's Spirit and transformed into a community of believers whose lives help create God's kingdom in this world. The "altar of sacrifice" (where victims died violent deaths) is transformed into a "communion table" (where the Father's family gathers to give thanks and praise with Jesus their brother).

> We are hungry and are fed. But there is still hunger. And so we must become the bread.
>
> Anonymous

This ritual perpetuation of our relationship with God no longer relies on bloody victims, but on the bloodless giving of Son and Father. Violence and victimization have no place at this table. Now it is a table of communion, a gift of our Father's love, our brother's total giving of his self so that we "may all be one. As you, Father, are in me and I am in you" (John 17:21).

This vision recognizes the encounter with our loving

Trinity as the only possibility of becoming who we are meant to be. It presents us with an unprecedented insight into who we are and who we can become. We are Christ's body. The Eucharist is the ritual integration of our unique relationship to God—to the Father through the Son, in the Holy Spirit. And our primary activity, our act of faith, is to surrender ourselves to transforming participation of this sacred meal. We are able to live differently because, now, we are different.

We live differently because we have a new identity. Now "it is no longer I who live, but it is Christ who lives in me" (Galatians 2:20). We are good, charitable, joyful, forgiving, reconciling, moral, just, wounded, limited, in need of each other, hungering for life-giving Bread, because we have allowed Divine Presence to be our source. Because we are loved unconditionally we can humbly know and accept ourselves for all of who we are. Because we are loved abundantly and mercifully, we can love others with compassionate love.

Letting Trinity Be Our Something

The ritual pattern of the Eucharist affords us a clear and consistent means to surrender ourselves to the Trinity's loving transformation of our lives. Think of all the different priests and styles of presiding at Mass that you have accepted over the years. I am sure there are some priests you like more than others, but for the most part, you have been able to accommodate yourself to a tremendous variety of styles. That means that in the Eucharist you have consistently practiced letting go of your expectations to be part of what is happening.

How many times have you left Mass thinking it was "boring" or "I didn't get anything out of it"? And yet you have returned. That is a form of letting go that is very close to contemplative prayer. In contemplative prayer you spend time in silence, just being with God. And good side effects come from it. You feel less stress, your blood pressure may lower, you feel a deep sense of self-confidence, and your overall health can improve.

None of these are the goal of prayer, and to make them a goal would distort your prayer, just as "trying to get something out of it" would distort the letting go that is the heart of our participation in the Eucharist. The point is not to "get something" but to be with God, to let Trinity be our "something." In the Eucharist we let go of our goals so that we can be with Trinity and one another. Because of that we become the change that is needed in the Father's kingdom.

> For through the law I died to the law, so that I might live to God. I have been crucified with Christ; and it is no longer I who live, but it is Christ who lives in me. And the life I now live in the flesh I live by faith in the Son of God, who loved me and gave himself for me.
>
> Galatians 2:19–20

Think about what we bring to the Eucharist. Our everyday lives are messy. Fatigue, personality conflicts, worries, ambitions, fears, time demands, and illness all crowd our awareness as we gather with others and all their different habits, expectations, and pious practices. Somehow we are all brought to a common ground. "Make the people sit down" Jesus told the disciples (John 6:10). And we do sit down—together.

When I began to focus on writing about the Eucharist, I knew I needed to learn more from people who have been on the front side of the altar for their whole lives. So I asked many of my friends to tell me, "What do you do during Mass?"

Not surprisingly, they do a lot of different things. Some say the rosary. Others focus on the gestures and ritual. Others listen for words and images that pique their interest. And still others devote themselves to joining in the responses.

I found this interesting because my response was so different. I found myself looking for "good" and "bad" liturgical practices, and I spent much time fantasizing about the changes I would make in these liturgies. I found it very frustrating to participate in a liturgy when the priest seemed to be going through the motions. I found that I was much more critical than any of my friends.

When I asked a friend, who does not seem the pious or devotional type, why he says the rosary when we should be praying as a community, he said, "It helps me to relax and just be there." After that I tried it for myself—not saying the rosary, but letting go and simply being there. What a wonderful difference.

To let go, to simply be here, now, with whatever is happening, sets the foundation for a more active and communal participation. Letting go is not a passive acceptance. It is an active attentiveness, a being present without judgments and prejudices.

The ritual pattern and immersion in God's ways are like a salve soothing our spirit to let go, surrender, let be. This is where we come with all our limitations to live for just a moment in the unlimited. Here, for a moment, we can see beyond the immediate and obvious to the meaningful and sacred.

Buddhists call this *mindfulness*. Theologians speak of reverence and contemplation. And Jesus tells us to be like little children. It is being present with fresh eyes. It is letting go of our judgments, and our criticisms, simply being present. And it is a tremendous relief—like coming out of a smoke-filled room into fresh air and sunlight, and feeling the wind blow around you as you take a deep breath.

> *The beginner's mind looks to find out what is new; it does not look to confirm. To look, we have to be ready to enter into the unknown. We have to be willing to throw away our armor of beliefs, knowledge, tradition, or whatever we cling to for comfort. We have to open up ourselves and be vulnerable. These are just ways of paying attention to the reality that is.*
>
> Kenneth S. Leong[11]

Stark, bare limbs of Winter
Laced in the pale budding green of Spring,
Lush with verdant Summer,
Giving way in the gilded rust of Autumn.
When judgment falls away,
Every moment is God's season.

Who We Are Because of Who God Is: Spirituality of the Eucharist

In the Eucharist we learn to integrate our true identity as the human/divine outpouring of the Trinity's love.

We are tutored in our identity as the beloved children of the Father, sisters and brothers to Jesus, who through the blessing of the Spirit are transformed into "my body broken...and my blood poured out" for the life of the world. We come as the human/divine mystery, with all its messiness and its sacred possibilities.

We are people of faith who start with material gifts, gifts that we can see and taste, smell, and feel. And we walk away as a spiritual gift. We are the ones who slowly digest this immense and intimate mystery in a ritual in which we celebrate, in the bread and the cup and retelling of Jesus' story, our becoming his flesh and blood in today's world.

In this ritual we give up and repeatedly let go to focus on the Father as our true possibility. In choosing to pray with a community we let go of our protective boundaries. In choosing to focus on our Father's agenda we lay our ego aside. In this letting go we receive the gift of our indescribable true self as a way of living and perceiving.

We are the people whose deepest longing for unconditional and eternal love is satisfied again and again until it seeps through all our defenses to melt our fears, anger, and anxiety and release our truest self, which is love and unobstructed awareness.

As the experience of our lives takes on meaning in the events of Jesus' living, dying, and rising we are transformed into the living body of Christ, creative partners in the Father's kingdom. We are the ones who become present to Jesus at the table of the Eucharist and become a sacrifice as we give up and let go of our little worlds to receive the gift of our true self. In this letting go, we come to a radical seeing-through, a new way of organizing and valuing the world of experiences. In this letting go, we are able to simply be here, now, with whatever is happening. This is an active attentiveness, a being present without judgments and prejudices. We are being cured of our blindness to see beyond the immediate and obvious to the meaning and sacredness of our lives.

Gathered around our Father's table with our sisters and brothers, we learn not to seek something from God but to let the Trinity be our "something."

Epilogue

Dear Friend,

I hope I am not being presumptuous, but if you have stayed with me this long, my hope is that we are both a little more aware that God has found heaven in our hearts.

I am also very much aware that new ideas, or a new insight, means very little until it informs our perception of our self, our identity, and slowly forms a new worldview, a new way of perceiving and relating to all that is. This is more than change; it is a transformation, a new way of being conscious. In the gospels this is called *repentance*.

Being part of a contemplative prayer group is immensely helpful. In the group to which I belong we sit together for a half-hour of silence, and we also share our experience of that silence. Sometimes there is a lot to share, sometimes there is very little or no desire to share. But the sharing, along with being together, sets the tone for my week.

This sharing is not meant to be advice. It is simply noticing our experience, but I find that it helps me become aware of nudgings that are so subtle that I overlook them. Since the group is made up of many different personalities, each with his or her unique sensitivity, we are enriched by one another's experience.

Even though I am highly introverted and more comfortable inside of myself rather than outside, this inner landscape, beyond the edges of my ego, is too daunting to explore alone. For all of us created in the image of Trinity it should not be a surprise that the bonding of this community is essential to our true selves.

In his book, *A Hidden Wholeness*, Parker J. Palmer says our true self (soul is the word he uses) is like a wild animal:

> *Like a wild animal, the soul is tough, resilient, resourceful, savvy, and self-sufficient: it knows how to survive in hard places...yet despite its toughness, the soul is also shy. Just like a wild animal, it seeks safety in the dense underbrush, especially when other people are around. If we want to see a wild animal, we know the last thing we should do is go crashing through the woods yelling for it to come out. But if we will walk quietly into the woods, sit patiently at the base of a tree, breathe with the earth, and fade into our surroundings, the wild creature we seek might put in an appearance. We may see it only briefly and only out the corner of an eye—but the sight is a gift we will always treasure as an end in itself.[1]*

His book is a tremendous resource for creating the kind of community that can establish a safe place for the soul/true self to show itself.

Our true self is very shy. We see its tracks, signs of its reality, but since it is us being aware, we can never gaze on our true self. That is why we need a community to act as a mirror. That also is why we need a community unlike any other we have experienced, a community created in silence, patience, and letting go. This type of community creates the sacred space needed for interior intimacy, and it creates the calm, quiet place where our true self feels at home.

Our true self is not going away. It is that gnawing emptiness that drives our desires. It is fierce in its attempts to take its rightful place as the center of our lives. It is that inner honesty that we are not being true to ourselves, and it leaves us uneasy and discontent with settling for less than we are. It is also that inner knowledge that perceives unconditionally, sees things as they are, and is indignant with our bigoted judgments and narrow-minded solutions.

I often wonder if the ego's best intentions aren't partly sabotaged by our true self holding out for the good of our entire being. Why is it that some intentions that we know are good and necessary—such as stopping smoking, losing weight, or consuming fewer resources—are so short-lived? Could our true self be holding out for learning to surrender and to love our whole self rather than impose the control of our ego?

I believe that our true self is also behind much of our loneliness. We are made for community, to connect deeply with others, to be loved in flesh and blood, to be love for others, and to be challenged beyond our small worlds by the beauty and variety of the Trinity's creation. As partners in the Trinity's kingdom we are the way this world becomes a better place for all creation.

Most of all, our true self wants to be life-giving, creative, and loving. We emerge from the heart of the Trinity, and our meaning is to give flesh and blood to our shared essence, to be the smile, the outstretched hand, the hug of belonging, the encouragement, and shared wisdom for one another.

The Child in the crib challenges us to love our whole self: human and divine. The cross where the Father and Son's hearts are laid bare; it brings us into the mystery of finding the Trinity's power in our helplessness. The Eucharist gives us the space to practice letting go, making room for the divine in simple earthy things such as bread and wine, and our brothers and sisters.

Let us humbly thank the Trinity for making our hearts home.

KEN SEDLAK, C.SS.R.

Sources

Every effort has been made to locate and secure permission for the inclusion of all copyrighted material in this book. If any such acknowledgments have been inadvertently omitted, the publisher would appreciate receiving full information so that proper credit may be given in future editions.

Introduction

1. Alphonsus Liguori, *The Way of Salvation.*

Chapter 1

1. Hildegard of Bingen, quoted in *Sacred Poems and Prayers of Love,* chosen by Mary Ford-Grabowsky (New York: Doubleday, 1998), 226.
2. Gerald G. May, *The Awakened Heart: Opening Yourself to the Love You Need* (San Francisco: HarperSan Francisco, 1993), 234.
3. Thomas Keating, *The Better Part: Stages of Contemplative Living* (New York: Continuum International Publishing Group, 2000), 57.
4. Ron Hanson, *Mariette in Ecstasy* (New York: Harper Perennial, 1992), 179.
5. May, *The Awakened Heart,* 31.
6. Meister Eckhart, in *Mysticism at the Dawn of the Modern Age.*
7. Thomas Merton, quoted in Beatrice Bruteau: *The Grand Option: Personal Transformation and a New Creation* (Notre Dame, IN: University of Notre Dame Press, 2001), 41.

8. Attributed to Dionysius the Areopagite in *Mystical Theology,* ch. 1.
9. St. Teresa of Ávila, in *Interior Castle,* IV, 1,9; quoted in Richard Rohr, *Everything Belongs: The Gift of Contemplative Prayer* (New York: Crossroad, 1999), 89.
10. May, *The Awakened Heart.*
11. Attributed to Saint Alphonsus Liguori, source unknown.

Chapter 2

1. Attributed to William McNamara, source unknown.
2. Eckhart Tolle, *The Power of Now: A Guide to Spiritual Enlightenment* (Novato, CA: New World Library, reprint edition, 2004), 171.
3. Anthony de Mello, *Awareness: A de Mello Spirituality Conference in His Own Words* (New York: Doubleday, 1990), 16, 27, 32, 73.
4. Meister Eckhart, in Sermon 12, as quoted in Anne Baring: *Individual Soul, Cosmic Soul and Spirit: A Working Model,* www.annebaring.com/anbar08_seminar12.htm.
5. May, *The Awakened Heart,* 234.
6. Dag Hammarskjold, *Markings* (New York: Ballantine, 1964), 151.
7. A. H. Almaas, *Essence with the Elixir of Enlightenment: The Diamond Approach to Inner Realization* (Boston: Weiser Books, 1998), 182.
8. John Shea, *Gospel Light: Jesus Stories for Spiritual Consciousness* (New York: Crossroad), 42.
9. John Kirvan, *There Is a God, There Is No God: A Companion for the Journey of Unknowing* (Notre Dame, IN: Sorin Books, 2003).
10. Anthony DeMello, on mysticism, http://www.katinka-hesselink.net/christianity/Anthony-de-mello-empty.html.

Chapter 3

1. Saint Alphonsus Liguori, from *The Selva* as quoted in H. Manders: "Love in the Spirituality of St. Alphon-

sus," transl. C. M. de Kuyer. *Readings in Redemptorist Spirituality,* Vol. 2, p. 46. (Published in "Apostolicum," March 1981).

2. Ernest Kurtz and Katherine Ketcham, *The Spirituality of Imperfection: Storytelling and the Journey to Wholeness* (New York: Bantam Books, 1994), 15.
3. Saint Teresa of Ávila; quoted in Beverly J. Lanzetta, *Radical Wisdom: A Feminist Mystical Theology* (Minneapolis, MN: Augsburg Fortress, 2005), 72–74.
4. Thomas Keating, *Healing Our Violence,* audiotape.
5. Eckhart Tolle, *The Power of Now, A Guide to Spiritual Enlightenment* (Novato, CA: New World Library, 1999), 121–45; also *A New Earth: Awakening to Your Life's Purpose* (New York: Dutton), 142–60.
6. Saint Alphonsus Liguori, from *The Selva* as quoted in H. Manders: "Love in the Spirituality of St. Alphonsus," transl. C. M. de Kuyer. *Readings in Redemptorist Spirituality,* Vol. 2. Published in "Apostolicum," March 1981.

Chapter 4

1. Excerpt from the Eucharistic Prayer in *The Sacramentary* (New York: Catholic Book Publishing, 1985), 545. © International Commission on English in the Liturgy.
2. Tony Hendra, *Father Joe, The Man Who Saved My Soul* (New York: Random House, 2004), 72.
3. Abraham Joshua Heschel, *God in Search of Man: A Philosophy of Judaism* (New York: Farrar, Straus and Giroux, 1976), 281.
4. Pierre Teilhard de Chardin, *Hymn of the Universe* (New York: HarperCollins, 1969), 23.
5. John S. Mogabgab, *Weavings.*
6. Attributed to Søren Kierkegaard, in *The Philosopher's Magazine on the Internet.* http://www.philosophers.co.uk/cafe/phil_sep2001.htm.
7. Mother Teresa of Calcutta, *Jesus, the Word to Be Spoken: Prayers and Meditations for Every Day of the Year*

(Cincinnati, OH: St. Anthony Messenger Press, 1998), 136.

8. Attributed to G. K. Chesterton.

9. Saint Augustine, *Sermon 272* (Minge, PI, vol 38, 1247), quoted from a translation by Joyce Ann Zimmermann, in *Liturgical Ministry*, 11 (2002): 100.

10. Mother Teresa of Calcutta, *A Gift for God* (New York: Harper Collins, 1996), 76.

11. Kenneth S. Leong, *The Zen Teachings of Jesus* (New York: Crossroad, 1998), 158

Epilogue

1. Parker J. Palmer, *A Hidden Wilderness: The Journey Toward an Undivided Life* (San Francisco: Jossey-Bass, 2004), 58.